Who Touched Me?

The War
For Your Body
Born of God

Jim Lynn

Order this book online at www.trafford.com
or email orders@trafford.com

Most Trafford titles are also available at major online book retailers.

Print information available on the last page.

ISBN: 978-1-6987-1606-0 (sc)
ISBN: 978-1-6987-1607-7 (e)

Library of Congress Control Number: 2023923772

Trafford rev. 12/19/2023

www.trafford.com
North America & international
toll-free: 844-688-6899 (USA & Canada)
fax: 812 355 4082

GodsHealingWord.org

God's Healing Word
Is an Online Christian Ministry Devoted
to Physical and Spiritual Healing in Christ.

Visit Our Website.
Subscribe to Our Free Newsletter.
GodsHealingWord.org

Praise the Lord, O my soul, and forget not
all His benefits – who forgives all your sins
and heals all your diseases.
- Psalm 103:3-4

Contents

Dedication

This Book is dedicated to elders and teachers in the Church, the Body of Christ. My prayer to God, our Father, is He bestows spiritual insight and wisdom on you, in reading and praying over this life-changing book.

Introduction

Healing Today in a Secular World

The information shared herein is given by faith
in a higher power over that of man.

The subject you are about to undertake is sadly not well-known nor taught in many churches. This vital subject is your Christian body's health as it relates to sin and God through Jesus Christ.

Before God created man, He created the plant kingdom. In doing so He placed everything mankind and animals would need to grow and maintain their physical health. And God called it good – Genesis 1:29-31.

When sin entered the world, the God given natural order of life changed. God cursed the earth because of man's sin - Genesis 3:17-19. Since that time up to present moment, all creation (i.e. earth) is groaning in agony waiting to be released from God's curse - Romans 8:19-22.

Here we are now some 6,000 years later after the fact, and boy howdy, look at all the sickness and disease in the world today (not to mention natural disasters and crime). As it relates to human health, commercial farms we depend on for plant nutrients to nourish our body no longer supply those needs. Over the years depletion of vital nutrients have disappeared from the soil due to poor farming practices, erosion, genetically modified seeds, and chemical fertilizers.

Years before, the soil that's being farmed now held 65 essential trace minerals vital for bodily health. Today, no more than 20 trace minerals can be found in farm soil. This is but one of several reasons why so many of us are sick. We're not getting the nutrition God requires for our body to maintain homeostasis (the ability of our body to keep itself in balance in order to fight infection, inflammation and disease).

There are, of course, other things we consume that keep our body out of homeostasis. (too much cane sugar, fast foods, tobacco, alcohol, pharmaceutical drugs, and now bio-engineered foods). However, quality food production is not the purpose of this study. That's because not every sickness and disease is due to lack of nutrition, or eating unhealthy foods.

God's Word tells us sin is also a cause of sickness and disease - Psalm 38:3-8. Associating sin with sickness is not an easy subject to discuss in Church (the Body of Christ), and so we avoid it. We avoid it because we're not suppose to live with sin in our lives, but we do - I John 1:8-10.

The primary sickness many of our brethren suffer from are chronic forms of illness, often-times a tell-tale marker that points to harboring sin. Since we do not talk about or discuss the subject of sin in our lives, few Christians are aware long-held sin can be the cause of chronic illness. This is not to say all forms of chronic illnesses originate from sin in our lives. Never-the-less, sin plays a major role in chronic illness (More on this later).

It is disease caused by our sins, and how and why the Gospel of Jesus Christ is all inclusive of healing sin-caused disease that this Bible study is undertaken.

Why The Statement on the Header of Every Page

Because we have the 1st Amendment: U.S. citizens who believe in a higher power, who hold to a spiritual belief, practice prayer and/or believe Holy Scripture, have a constitutional right to uphold and practice their beliefs without hindrance from governmental regulation, rule, or law. This includes healing the sick.

The FDA, CDC, NIH and every other three letter bureaucratic agency within the U.S. Government is secular in nature. That is to say many of those with bureaucratic powers are led by the sinful nature of this world (power, greed, love of money, position, control). Those agencies in charge of overseeing our health will not honor our constitutional rights, unless we claim them. So be prepared to defend your rights and spiritual beliefs, or lose them to the powers of this world. There is nothing new about this struggle. What makes the winning difference is knowledge!

"Knowledge will forever govern ignorance: And a
people who mean to be their own Governors, must arm
themselves with the power which knowledge gives."
- James Madison, 1798

Those words from James Madison, the 4th President of the United States, are as true today as when our nation was in its infancy. If we do not empower ourselves with knowledge, we will lose our freedoms to tyranny.

"My people are destroyed from lack of knowledge."
- Hosea 4:6

The Legal Difference is One of Setting and Intent.

For example: Whenever two or more people of faith come together in the name of Jesus Christ, Matthew 18:20 tells us Jesus is there with them. This establishes a spiritual setting and intent allowing them to practice their faith. First, to declare God's Glory, repentance, and the power of prayer. Secondly, to declare healing belongs to God. And three, to declare the godly healing power of plants for use in healing the sick in the name of the Lord.

Conversely, whenever two or more people come together in a secular setting, their speech and practices as it relates to making health claims are bound by bureaucratic regulation. Again, the difference is one of setting and intent. The first is spiritual. The second is secular. The first is protected by the 1st Amendment, The second apparently is not. So you know, the word "secular" literally means "without God."

Healing Belongs to God, Not Man!

The one word missing from all secular medical and government terminology related to treating the sick is the word **heal**. Ever wonder why? Healing belongs to God alone, not man. Simply, this explains why no doctor has ever healed anyone from disease without God's hand at work. Period!

Exodus 15:26 states, "...For I am the Lord, who heals you." Translate that verse however you will, it means it is God, and God alone, who heals. It applies universally to all mankind. More importantly, Exodus 15:26 not only tells us what God does, but also who God is. The original biblical Hebrew text of Exodus 15:26 reads: "For I am **Yahweh-Rapha**." That word, Yahweh-Rapha, is a proper noun describing who God is. In other words, Yahweh-Rapha describes God's nature and being. Healing is not just something He does, it's part of who God is.

Old Testament declarative words that describe God's nature:

YAHWEH-RAPHA:.........The Lord Who Heals..... - Exodus 15:26
YAHWEH-JIREH:..........The Lord will Provide... - Genesis 22:14

YAHWEH-NISSI:...............The Lord Our Banner - Exodus 17:15
YAHWEH-M'KADDESH:..The Lord Who Sanctifies - Leviticus 20:8
YAHWEH-SHALOM:.........The Lord Our Peace - Judges 6:24
YAHWEH-ROHI:...............The Lord Our Shepherd - Psalm 23:1
YAHWEH-SABAOTH:.......The Lord of Hosts - Psalm 46:7
JEHOVAH-TSIDKENU:....The Lord Our Righteousness– Jer. 23:6

Notice each of the above declarative statements are found in the Old Testament. Why is that? Because it is in the Old Testament where God reveals His nature to man, who He is, what faith is and how it works, what holiness is and so much more. I mention this only because it is usually <u>New Testament Christians unfamiliar with the Old Testament who are the ones most likely to stray or struggle in their faith.</u> The New Testament is confirmation of the Old Testament revealed in the fullness of time.

So God is our healer, not man. This is why in a secular setting you'll hear the word "cure" used instead of "heal." Physicians legally cannot use the word "heal." The word cure (in today's legal world) means "to cover up or to eliminate symptoms." By contrast, the word heal means "to save or make whole." The differences between the two are like night and day. Think about it. Would you rather be healed or cured?

So at the heart of it all, physical healing is an event that originates with God in the spiritual realm. This is why no doctor can ever say, "I healed her of cancer." He may or may not have "treated" her for cancer, but it is Yahweh-Rapha who healed her.

Setting And Intent is Key to Healing in a Legal, Secularized World.

Some may question whether the Church and individual believers have a legal right to practice healing. After all, our society has laws structured to prevent non-licensed individuals to practice medicine. The answer is **yes!** The Church and Her membership has every legal authority to heal the sick but not to practice medicine. Understanding the difference between the two allows the Church and believers to legally heal the sick without the need for a medical license.

Allopathic medicine is engaged in the treatment of sickness and disease. It exists solely for the purpose of legally offering diagnosis, prescription, treatment, and containment of disease. Healing is not its agenda or end purpose. It may appear to be so to the uninformed, but it is not.

To protect its interests, laws are in place to shelter the medical industry, all in the public interest of safety of course. It is unlawful for medically unlicensed individuals to diagnose, to prescribe, or to treat people afflicted with illness. It is unlawful to "play" doctor by using certain terminology controlled by the medical industry. Words like "treatment," "diagnose," "cure," "disease," and "recommend" are all words protected by law when used in connection with illness and disease. Unlicensed people can be fined and imprisoned for using such language.

However, while there are laws to prevent the public from "playing" doctor, there are no laws held against the public for healing the sick. Healing is free of man's constraints. So...

Understanding the difference between healing the sick and treating the sick is the difference between keeping the law and breaking it.

The Church functions by divine authority. It does not require man's authority to do so. Likewise, health and healing belong to God, not man. We are fortunate in the U.S. To have Constitutional rights permitting freedom of religion. Therefore, healing ministries are fully protected by the First Amendment to the Constitution of the United States. Churches and individuals are free to engage in healing the sick using God's spiritual model without interference from government. But even if they were not free to do so, God's law of the Spirit of Life supersedes the laws of mankind.

Our Words Make All The Difference.

A simple proclamation of faith to a higher power can empower you from being subject to the FDA Health Claim Rule. It provides the reader with information by whose authority you make your claim, and allows him or her to make a decision based on faith, rather than on a rule of man. It also informs government authority of which setting and intent you are focused on (secular or spiritual). Before you speak or write, declare a proclamation of faith to establish setting and intent. This proclamation can be simple, upfront and to the point. For example:

> "The information shared herein is given by faith
> in a higher power over that of man."

This is why you see the above statement on the headers of this study. Readers will know the structure and intent of this study is Godly, not secular. By including such a statement in our work and ministry, we may also speak of personal and anecdotal testimonials (giving God the glory and credit) without fear of reprisal. To keep the integrity of our faith intact we will want to avoid the appearance of propriety. We may, however, offer resources of natural products and call them by name when those products are made unique by formulation.

Chapter one

Your Body Born of God

> He came to that which was his own,
> but his own did not receive him. Yet to
> all who did receive him, to those who
> believed in his name, he gave the right
> to become children of God — **children
> born not of natural descent, nor of
> human decision or a husband's will,
> but born of God.**
>
> - John 1:11-13

This Bible study is about your God-given body. No, not the body you were physically born with: Rather your body born of God when you became a Christian. There's a big difference between the two.

Before getting into this study, please know it's my love for God's holy Word and the Church, the Body of Jesus Christ, that this study was undertaken. It's purpose is to draw us closer, with understanding, to what God has provided us, His children. I also want to assure readers this study comes only after years of studying what God's Word tells us, and measured against modern day church doctrine and teaching. With that let's begin.

Prior to obeying the Gospel your physical body was carnal (soulish), and ruled over by spiritual forces of evil – I Corinthians 2:14. In your re-birth into Christ, your physical body was spiritually re-born of God. Even though your body is subject to death because of sin, Your new spiritual, physical body in Christ is now ruled over by the Spirit from God to give eternal life to your now mortal body – Romans 8:9-11.

It's important you understand the difference between carnal bodies and spiritual bodies. A carnal body is ruled over by Satan. A spiritual body is ruled over by God. While Satan easily rules over carnal bodies, he is especially at war with God to rob Him of our spiritual bodies born of God. One way he does this is by duping Christians (often through church doctrine) to believe God no longer heals the sick like they read in the New Testament. The net affect of this teaching is many Christians lose their faith in the God of healing to heal their physical body from sickness and disease; and so turn back to the world for healing they didn't find in their faith.

God created man to be a 3 part being, comprised of a physical body, a spirit, and soul. It's not that man has a body, has a spirit, and a soul. Man is only man when these 3 dwell together as a one (man = body, spirit, soul - Genesis 2:7). Death destroys man's soul by separating his body from his spirit – Ecclesiastes 12:7, Acts 7:59, Luke 23:46. When body and spirit are reunited, man becomes a living soul once again. The Apostle Paul explained it this way...

> You, however, are not in the realm of the flesh but are in the realm of the Spirit, if indeed the Spirit of God lives in you. And if anyone does not have the Spirit of Christ, they do not belong to Christ. But if Christ is in you, then even though

> your body is subject to death because of sin, the Spirit gives life because of righteousness. **And if the Spirit of him who raised Jesus from the dead is living in you, he who raised Christ from the dead will also give life to your mortal bodies because of his Spirit who lives in you**.
> - Romans 8:9-11

It's essential you understand just how important your physical body is to God. For we were born (created) in the image and likeness of God through Jesus Christ, our Lord and Savior, to live with Him as we were created. Because of sin, God's plan of redemption (The healing Gospel of Christ) preserves our being in body, spirit, and soul for eternity – I Thessalonians 4:13-17.

If you believe we are created in the image and likeness of God – Genesis 2:7, you must also believe Jesus today lives in heaven as a flesh and blood human being.

> For there is one God and one mediator between God and men, the MAN Christ Jesus.
> - I Timothy 2:5

The word MAN in the original Greek text is written in the present tense. In other words, Jesus lives in heaven in His (glorified) flesh for eternity. Stop and think what this means for you and yours. Our flesh will one day become glorified as His flesh is.

Healing and The Resurrection of Jesus Christ.

Now it may come as a surprise to some readers, but there are those in our brotherhood who do NOT believe they will keep

3

their fleshly bodies in the resurrection from the dead. They cite I Corinthians 15:50 written by the Apostle Paul.

> "I declare to you, brothers, that flesh and blood cannot inherit the kingdom of God, nor does the perishable inherit the the imperishable."

So what did Paul mean when he said, "flesh and blood cannot inherit the kingdom of God (verse 50)?" Taken on the surface, it would seem that Paul is defending the notion of the dual nature of man. But is this correct? And what exactly is the difference between a natural body and a spiritual body?

Let me say from the out-start <u>we will keep our bodies</u> in the resurrection, but not as we know them now. <u>They will be changed, not exchanged</u>. I'll explain because without a correct understanding of the resurrection, one cannot understand how it is possible that Christ heals sickness today.

Christians who do not believe in a bodily resurrection of the dead often quote the above verse. In doing so, they incorrectly interpret flesh and blood as substance (man's body) rather than a state of being. Let me explain.

The term "flesh and blood" is used frequently throughout Scripture. It is an old Jewish expression which refers to man as he is now: Weak, frail, and subject to corruption, sin, decay, and death. Used in I Corinthians 15, it is not the substance (the physical body) that Paul has in mind but rather what "flesh and blood" represent. Some biblical examples of flesh and blood... Matthew 16:17, Galatians 1:15-16, Hebrews 2:14 (Your Bible version may say man instead of flesh and blood. However the original texts all use "flesh and blood" instead of man).

So when Paul uses the term "flesh and blood" in I Corinthians 15, all he is saying is that which is perishable and corrupt cannot enter into the spiritual realm of God. This understanding aligns itself with Paul's insistence of a physical

4

resurrection. The inspired Apostle was not satisfied for the Church to believe in life beyond the grave. He insisted upon a resurrection of our spiritual, physical bodies, and so must we.

The resurrection of our physical bodies is the hope of man. For without his flesh, man ceases to be man (a living soul). Our bodies will be changed (not exchanged) in the resurrection - I Corinthians 15:51. In the transformation (glorification) that takes place, our glorified flesh will be reunited with our departed spirits to become living souls (man) once again - I Thessalonians 4:13-18. Our resurrected, glorified fleshly body will no longer be subject to sin, sickness, disease or corruption of any kind. This is the ultimate healing, the hope that sustains us - Philippians 3:21.

If man is to "escape" his fleshly body in death, as taught by the early Greeks and believed as some Christians do today, Christ suffered and died in vain. But God's Scheme of Redemption includes our body as well as our spirit. Without the physical, bodily resurrection of Jesus Christ from the grave, our faith is in vain; and our sins are still before us - I Corinthians 15:17.

So how did this twisted teaching gain such a large following? And what would it mean to the mission of the Church if the true message of I Corinthians 15 were understood?

During the days of the Apostle Paul, there existed a school of thought in Greece (Gnosticism) that taught all flesh is inherently evil; that our human spirit will be freed of its earthly prison (the body) in death. Central to this thinking is the ancient Greek belief of the dual nature of man. This belief held that man's body is of a lower nature and is a trap for the soul. The spirit, or soul, was considered the higher nature of man and longed to be free of the material body. Paul wrote to the saints in the Church at Corinth on the matter because there were believers there who were swayed to this agnostic teaching.

Today, though many Christians have not thought it through completely, they agree with this ancient agnostic view of man. This dual concept of man then sets the foundation to treat the body apart from the soul today; and explains much of our

5

dependence on secular medicine rather than on God's Word for healing. It also helps to explain why so few churches have healing ministries. In short, they either do not believe in the bodily resurrection of the dead, or in divine healing today. Hence, no healing ministries.

The Letter from the Apostle Paul to the Church at Corinth -I Corinthians 15, dispels the dual nature of man and re-affirms, with emphatic insistence, the physical resurrection of man's fleshly body from the grave. For it was in Corinth where this agnostic teaching against the physical resurrection of human flesh took place (verse 12).

Note: While our fleshly body must die (temporarily), our spirit does not: It returns to God – Ecclesiastes 12:7, John 11:26, I Thessalonians 4:13-17.

I Corinthians 15 (The Resurrection is The Foundation of Christian Belief)

The resurrection of Jesus' body from the grave is the foundational truth of Christianity. Without it, we are all hopelessly lost. Because Gnosticism was creeping into the Church in Corinth, Paul wrote to the Church refuting Gnosticism, saying in effect, "How can some of you believe the Gospel (verses 1-4) we preached to you and not believe in the resurrection of your body one day (verses 12-17)?"

The resurrection of the human body is the key message of the Christian faith –Acts 2:23-24, 26:8. The age-old question of whether man will live again - Job 14:14, is answered through the resurrection of Jesus Christ. Jesus declared a time is coming when all who are in their graves will come out and walk upright - John 5:28-29. There is to be a judgment. Those who have received the gift of the Holy Spirit – Acts 2:38, have placed their faith in Christ and have repented from their sins will rise to live - I John 3:2-3. Those who have lived in sin will rise to condemnation.

For Christians, life from the grave begins now through belief in Jesus Christ - John 7:38, 10:10. God heals man from the inside out in preparation for man's physical body to be glorified in the resurrection - II Corinthians 4:16; Philippians 3:21. We are recreated inwardly through our second birth which is spiritual - John 3:5-8.

This bible study is also critical of some Christians today who do not consider or believe the body they live in now is spiritual. They reason their bodies are physical and mortal, so how can anything that is physical be spiritual?

This is why Bible study is so important; so we can know the truth and grow in our faith. To wit, the bread God rained down on Jewish exiles was real physical bread; yet at the same time was spiritual, because God sent it to them - Exodus 16:4, I Corinthians 10:2-3. The Apostle Paul calls believers spiritual – I Corinthians 2:15, Galatians 6:1. This includes our physical, born again body.

I mention this because the spiritual issues in today's Christian Church concerning our physical body are similar to the issues the Corinthian Church faced. They literally dismissed the flesh and blood body of Jesus in their born again bodies and lives. The Apostle Paul corrected them saying...

> Do you not know that your (flesh and bone) bodies are members of Christ himself?
> - I Corinthians 6:15

> ...Do you not realize that Christ Jesus is in you—Unless of course you fail the test?
> - II Corinthians 13:5

And to the Ephesians he wrote:

> For we are members of His body
> (original text reads "of his flesh and
> of his bones"). For this reason a man
> will leave his father and mother and
> be united to his wife, and the two will
> become one flesh. This is a profound
> mystery – but I am talking about Christ
> and the church.
>
> - Ephesians 5: 30-32

From the above verses, it should be obvious the flesh of your Christian body is spiritually made one with the flesh of Jesus Christ. I say obvious because God's Word makes it obvious. His Body and your body are spiritually one flesh. Praise God!!!

So I ask: Have you ever considered this amazing truth and what it means for your health, both physically and spiritually? Some questions to consider:

If the Body of Jesus lives in you,

- why would you ever become chronically ill?
- why would you look to the world for healing?
- what are you forgetting in taking the Lord's Supper?
- what does that say about your body's resurrection?
- why doesn't your church teach this truth?

As to that last question, the lack of this teaching explains why so many of our brethren are chronically ill and live their lives the way they do. It also explains why so many congregations lack growth. More on this later.

Honor God With Your Body.

> Do you not know that your body is a
> temple (shrine) of the Holy Spirit, who

8

> is in you, whom you have received from
> God? **You are not your own. You were**
> **bought with a price. Therefore honor**
> **God with your body.** - I Cor. 6:19-20

There it is! <u>You are not your own</u>. Your one time carnal body is now a spiritual body. Your body was purchased by Jesus Christ, the sinless Lamb of God who carried, possessed all our (your) sins, sicknesses, and sorrows on the cross, so that those born of God may be healed in body, spirit, and soul. - Psalm 103: 3, Isaiah 53:3-5, I Peter 2:24

As I write this in the Fall of 2023, Satan, the prince of earth, is making a full frontal attack on our God-given bodies. Our world seemingly is being over-run with...

Transgenderism
Lesbianism
Homosexuality
Pornographic books in government elementary schools
Churches celebrating drag queens
Government sponsored Gay Pride Month
Mind altering drugs
Dependency on pharmaceutical drugs (See Chapter 3)
Unnecessary surgeries and medications

These are all sinful acts which directly attack the body. It makes no difference if that body is carnal or born of God. And while those evils have always been in the world, the focus on them seemingly has never been more open or prevalent. It's as though advocates of these forms of sin are purposely pushing their lifestyle on society.

But Satan doesn't stop with influencing and destroying carnal bodies. He is especially after our spiritual body in Christ to discourage our faith. As stated earlier, he does this with Church doctrine that often leaves out (overlooks) the blessings of good health that come with obeying the Gospel.

> We have not received the spirit from the world, but the Spirit who is from God, that we may understand what God has freely given us. - I Corinthians 2:12

One of the greatest gifts God gives us is His love expressed through good health in our body, and healing when we fall ill. For He is not only our creator, He is also **Yahweh-Rapha** (Hebrew for "I am the Lord who heals you"). - Exodus 15:26

Sadly, in our brotherhood today, we have lost God's name (who He is). Our general teaching today is God no longer heals the sick like we read about in the Bible. We teach the healing performed by Jesus and His Apostles in the New Testament was to prove the authenticity of their message. Without question this was so, but misses the main point of the Good News....**God is our Healer** (both physically and spiritually)...Not for once upon a time, but for all time and eternity - Psalm 103:2-4.

Why Many Christians Suffer With Chronic Illness

When the Apostle Paul learned many Christians in Corinth were suffering with sickness and early death, he wrote to them and told them why.

> A man ought to examine himself before he eats of the bread and drinks of the cup. **For everyone who eats and drinks without recognizing the body, eats and drinks judgment on himself. That is why many among you are weak and**

sick, and a number of you have have fallen asleep. - I Corinthians 11:28-30

Notice how Paul binds the physical well-being of our fleshly body directly to acknowledgment of the fleshly body of Jesus in the Lord's Supper. The Church in Corinth had faith Jesus willingly shed His blood for the forgiveness of sin. What they lacked is knowing faith (belief) in the healing power of the Lord's fleshly body to heal (make whole) their fleshly bodies... "by His wounds we are healed" - Isaiah 53:3-5. This is what we are to remember in taking the Lord's Supper: What was being overlooked by many believers in the Corinthian Church. Paul told them:

> "That is why many among you are weak and sick, and a number of you have fallen asleep."

Now I did not say that: The inspired Apostle Paul did!

For Christians today, we need to be reminded there are two realities contained in observance of the Lord's Supper. One is the shedding of Jesus' blood for atonement of sin – Hebrews 9:22. The other is Jesus' sacrifice of His fleshy body for healing. For it is through His stripes (His suffering and torment in the flesh) that we can be physically healed today – Psalm 103:3, Isaiah 53:5; I Peter 2:24.

Said another way: Without Jesus' body broken and torn flesh, there could be no healing of any kind, either before or after the Cross. This includes all life here on earth. I believe this is where many Christians today lack discernment - Romans 11:36; Colossians 1:15-18. It is Jesus' physical bodily resurrection from His grave that empowers our bodies to heal from sickness.

Throughout his many letters, Paul relates the relationship of our fleshly body to the fleshly body of Jesus Christ as being members of His body (one flesh). Celebrating the Lord's Supper can either provide or deny us healing by how we accept or deny the divine healing power of the fleshly, glorified body of Jesus Christ living in us.

The cup represents His blood. The bread represents His body. If we come to the Lord's Supper and partake of the cup and the bread, but we deny His bodily wounds as part of the Gospel for healing - Isaiah 53:5; we forsake the love God offers us for Jesus to be our healer...apart from salvation. For that reason, should we eliminate His broken body and resurrection as the power for healing, even though we celebrate His fleshly body by eating the bread, we bring judgment unto ourselves.

It is for this reason many of us are inflicted with disease and insanity today, because we have said in our heart that it (miraculous, divine, spiritual, providential, or any other name we wish to call God's healing) passed away two thousand years ago: Yet we still participate in the Lord's Supper which represents its reality for today.

Said another way: While we recognize (have faith in) the blood of Jesus Christ to save our souls, we do not recognize (have faith in) His literal body to heal our literal bodies of disease—here—now (Even though our fleshly body is one flesh with His body).

I know for many in the Body of Christ this presents a new teaching which some will struggle with to reconcile. My purpose is to teach God's Word as truthfully and as honestly as I can without prejudice. It is the same for any minister, teacher or elder in our number. And, we do not do so to cause dissension or to be argumentative, but to uphold and strengthen our faith and the faith of our brethren.

The struggle is not so much with God's Word. The struggle lies in our recognizing and accepting what the Word teaches. That is certainly not new, but I mention it here for two reasons:

1. We struggle to fully understand our relationship with Jesus Christ as both a man and as God.

2. We struggle to accept (believe) and receive the benefit of His power in our lives here on earth.

Paul is telling us there is more to the Lord's Supper than remembering His blood sacrifice for the forgiveness of our sins – Hebrews 9:22. Jesus also sacrificed His Body for life and physical healing to be possible - Isaiah 53: 3-5, John 6:51. Yet, have you ever heard this truth spoken prior to taking the Lord's Supper? For many, never!

The lack of this essential teaching today leads to the failure of understanding:

A. How righteousness (sanctification) affects our body physically with health.
B. How sin affects our body physically with chronic forms of disease.

Yes, both sin and righteousness affect our physical bodies. Righteousness leads to good health and longevity, while sin leads to many forms of chronic illness and death before our ordained time - Psalm 139:16.

Are Thoughts and Emotions Physical or Spiritual?

Consider and think this through carefully: Are the thoughts and emotions that rule your actions physical or spiritual in nature? If you believe that the essence of life is physical and that thoughts and emotions are based on and governed by the physical realm because we live in a physical world, then Satan already has you in his camp. But if you believe that the essence of life is spiritual and that thoughts and emotions are based on and governed by the spiritual realm, then you realize your full worth as a spiritual being of God's creation.

Understanding that life is a spiritual experience, lived out in a physical world, is crucial to understanding why all healing is spiritual. If Satan can get you to believe that any or all healing is merely a manifestation of the physical realm, you are in great danger.

Friends, we are spiritual beings, lock, stock, and barrel. Even the physical body in which we dwell is spiritual and subject to God. We bear His very likeness - Genesis 1:26. and belong to Him as His own - Psalm 100:3. We are God's greatest love and most valued possession. We were created to be with God, to dwell with Him.

Satan, who could care less about us as individuals, wants only to rob God by keeping us separated from our heavenly Father. He (Satan) will do anything to foster doubt in God or to foil God's work, including assaults on our body - Job 1:6-12. Thus, there is a great spiritual war at work between the forces of heaven and hell to determine who will possess us, God or Satan - Ephesians 6:12.

The battleground of this spiritual war lies within each of us. This is the reason why God tells us to test the spirits to see if they are from God -1 John 4:1-6, and we are not feeble or unable to defend ourselves because God offers us His protective armor - Ephesians 6:10-18.

God knows that failure to recognize the presence of Satan in our Christian life plays directly into Satan's hand. Satan's weapons in this war are fear, worry, greed, lust, jealousy, hatred, guilt, unforgiveness, low self-esteem and the like. These are the spiritual weapons of evil that can separate us from God. But though they be spiritual in nature, these weapons manifest their presence physically in our lives in many ways, including our body. That we suffer in body with chronic illness and in spirit with mental anguish is sure sign of the war within us - Ephesians 6:12.

God created us perfectly, but sin changes us. Every thought we have, be it good or bad, produces a chemical and neurological response within our body. So long as our beliefs have their origin in a loving spirit, the response in our body helps to maintain homeostasis (balance). When the origin of our belief originates from an unloving spirit, the response creates imbalance in our body, and we become sickly if we accept and live the lie. So how is this so?

Your body's hypothalamus is a vital gland of the limbic system. The limbic system is what science refers to as the mind/body connection. In healing ministries we refer to it as the spirit, soul, body connection - I Thessalonians 5:23.

Expressions of fear, stress, worry, tension, panic, anger, guilt, greed, lust, and many other forms of sin are facilitated and acted upon by the hypothalamus gland. This is the gland that responds to you emotionally and spiritually. It physically produces what is happening within your heart, soul and spirit.

Gerard J. Tortora, author of Principles of Anatomy, states the following about our hypothalamus:

> "The hypothalamus represents the physical connection between soul and body. Everything that concerns thought (be it good or bad) travels through the hypothalamus, and thus through the rest of the body. And so it is, all our thoughts are connected (be they holy or evil) and given expression in the physiological part of our lives. Just as fear can be the cause of illness, peace can be the cause of homeostasis."

Terry Shepherd Friedmann, M.D., author of Freedom Through Health states;

> "The emotions such as fear, anger, hatred, jealousy, envy, and prejudices kill the spirit and, hence, the very nature of man. The person who is filled

with emotions such as these is sick physically, mentally, and spiritually. For example, patients who were more fixed in their thought and behavior patterns often suffered from arthritis. Rigidity in thoughts created inflexibility in the body...Patients who had difficulty expressing love and other personal feelings had blocked coronary arteries."

Also from my ministry I've learned fear-caused anxiety often causes asthma. Great anger against ones self develops high cholesterol. Breast cancer is often a coming out of the sin of conflict and bitterness between a female and another close female (mother, daughter, sister).

Satan is very clever. He knows our every weakness and attacks us where we are most vulnerable. He knows his unloving spirit (weapons) can destroy our body and discourage our faith in God.

Have you ever personally considered the association between deeply seated emotions and chronic forms of illness? Psychologists believe about 80% of chronic illnesses originate from one or more of these emotions when they are allowed to dominate and rule over our life? Amazing!

These harmful emotions not only make people sick, they kill the human spirit (who we are as human beings). Chronic illness and disease of all sorts, from arthritis, asthma, bipolar disorder, bronchitis, cancer, depression, epilepsy, heart disease, high blood pressure, ulcerative colitis, crohn's disease, lupus, and many more all owe their due to Satan. Hundreds of millions of people needlessly bear a wide assortment of these illnesses everyday.

What the World Calls Psychosomatic, God Calls an Unclean Spirit.

God's Word tells us when we turn our lives over to Christ and repent of our sins, it is our prayers through our love and faith in Jesus for physical healing and wellness that physical healing begins in the body. Dr. Friedmann in speaking of the positive healing power of love states:

> "When love (agape) is openly given to others, miracles can happen. There is a complete lack of judgment here. We know judgment of others, as well as self, can limit health and healing and create blocks of negative emotion. Anger, fear, and guilt are some of the more destructive emotions, These cause blocks in the natural energy flow of the body that can ultimately lead to breakdown and disease, the opposite of this is love and the expression of it. Love is the most powerful healing modality on earth today.

God's spiritual weapon to redeem us from evil is love—love not as the world knows it, but love as only that which comes from God - John 3:16; I John 4:16. It is God's love, expressed through Jesus Christ, that empowers us to conquer Satan, to find God, health, and life. Love conquers evil, demonstrated in the physical and mental anguish suffered by Jesus during His trial and execution - Isaiah 53:4-5. Love is the exact opposite of all that evil stands for and is all powerful - I Corinthians 13. It is love that heals the body, spirit, and soul for those of us wounded by Satan's arrows.

The spiritual problem that exists today is many Church leaders do not associate sin (unclean spirits) with sickness and disease. However the Psalmist, David, knew exactly why he suffered in body: It was the price he paid for his sins. He wrote:

> Because of your wrath there is no health in my body. **My bones have no soundness because of my sin**...My wounds fester and are loathsome because of my sinful folly...My back is filled with searing pain; **there is no health in my body**. =Psalm 38: 3-8

The wisest man of old, King Solomon, also had something to say about sin and sickness (Notice especially how both men associate sin with bone health).

> Do not be wise in your own eyes; **fear the Lord and shun evil. This will bring health to your body and nourishment to your bones.**
> - Proverbs 3: 7-8

> **A heart at peace gives life to the body,** but **envy rots the bones**.
> - Proverbs 14:30

> **A Cheerful heart is good medicine, but a crushed spirit dries up the bones.**
> - Proverbs 17:22

> My son, pay attention to what I say; listen closely to my words. Do not let them out of your sight, keep them within your heart; for **they are life to those**

who find them and health to a man's whole body. - Proverbs 4: 20-22

Ever wonder why both David and King Solomon would tie sin and sickness to bone health? You are probably aware of the fact that you have "red blood cells" and "white blood cells" in your blood. The white blood cells are probably the most important part of your immune system. And it turns out that "white blood cells" are actually a whole collection of different cells that work together to destroy bacteria and viruses.

All white blood cells are known officially as **Leukocytes**. White blood cells are not like normal cells in the body - they actually act like independent, living single-cell organisms able to move and capture things on their own. White blood cells behave very much like amoeba in their movements and are able to engulf other cells and bacteria. Many white blood cells cannot divide and reproduce on their own, but instead have a factory somewhere in the body that produces them. **That factory is the bone marrow** within our bones.

Mind you, David and Solomon lived some 3,500 ago. They most likely knew nothing about red or white blood cells, but they knew what happens to the human body when sin enters our lives.

How is it today, having God's completed written word, so many of our brethren lack this inspired knowledge? Could it be we need to rely more on God's Word than we do church doctrine? I ask because there is only one inspired Word of God (the Bible), while there are hundreds of church doctrines.

> All Scripture is God-breathed and is useful for teaching, rebuking, correcting, and training in righteousness, so that the servant of God may be thoroughly equipped for every good work.
> - II Timothy 3:16-17

Salvation and Sanctification:

The books of Matthew, Mark, Luke, John, and the book of Acts demonstrate God's love (salvation and healing) through Jesus Christ, the Apostles and the early Church. From the books of Romans to Jude, God teaches us about sanctification.

As a people of God we are taught much about the Good News, the Gospel of Christ, but very little about His Spirit of discernment and the consequence of sin in our lives.

Take King David of the Old Testament for example. The Bible says David was a man after God's own heart. God loved David greatly. But David had unresolved sin in his life, which left him sick and miserable. God did not heal David until David faced his sin and repented. David wrote: "O Lord...Because of your wrath there is no health in my body; my bones have no soundness because of my sin" - Psalm 38:3.

David recognized the relationship between sin and sickness and had to sanctify his life (to repent of his sin and strive to live a holy life that imitates the nature of God) before God healed him. It is no different for us today. God requires we sacrifice (turn away from sin); to live a life of holiness before He will heal our body from sickness.

Sacrifice means there will be a struggle within our heart and soul. Yes, we live by God's grace knowing our sins are covered by the blood of Jesus, both past and future; but that does not mean we are free to live in sin as a way of life. For by doing so we remain a slave to sin – Romans 6:1-2.

Do you feel you are a slave to worry, anger, jealousy? Let me say that another way. Do you live with worry, anger, guilt? If so, you have issues you need to ask God for help to overcome. Now everyone has worries. However, when worry becomes an all consuming aspect of our life...when we lose sleep or can't eat because our heart and soul are so preoccupied with worry, that is sin.

Why? Because those consumed by worry are still sitting on their own throne. They want to be in control of their lives. They may pay lip service to God, but if worry preoccupies their mind, that's the nature of a soulish, natural man…a man or woman whose life is not led by the Spirit of God.

A Spirit led man or woman will worry, but they are quick to give worry up to God. Instead of carrying worry, they turn to God in Prayer for help with life's problems. They are at peace. Mind you, this is not merely an exercise, but a genuine release. How can this be? These people have crucified their lives. They have been crucified with Christ and no longer live, but Christ lives in them. The life they live in the body, they live by faith in the Son of God – Galatians 2:20.

In the chart below, I visualize the walk of a spirit led man. That jagged line represents our walk (our life) in Christ after obeying the Gospel. It illustrates our life-long spiritual battle with temptation, sin, and repentance as we grow in sanctification.

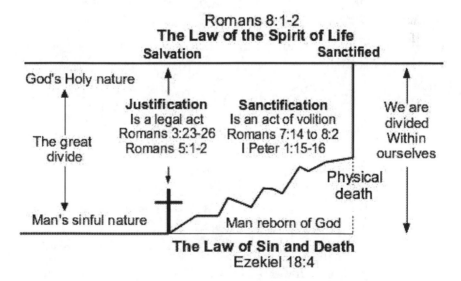

Think of salvation and sanctification in this manner: The act of salvation is a legal act, something performed on you.

Sanctification is an act of volition, something you voluntarily do yourself with the help of God's Spirit.

Again, when you were saved, you were "justified" - Romans 3:23-26. Justification simply means Jesus paid the penalty for your sins, past present and future. You did nothing yourself to be justified, other than to believe and have faith. But nothing happened in being saved to keep you that way. You are still the same free-will person with the faults you had before you were saved.

After the cross you are to grow in the Lord spiritually by removing sin that may be still part of your life (See James 5:13-16). This is called sanctification, growing in holiness - I Thessalonians 5:23. **Sanctification is a life-long process**, not a one time event. In the end, God will not judge your faith by your perfection (holiness) or lack of it, but rather by your walk (spiritual growth) in the Lord – I John 1:8 to 2:2.

Many Christians today believe because they are born again that they cannot sin, but The Bible tells it differently. If you suffer in body, rest assured that sin is close at hand. The Apostle Paul struggled with sin in his life. Some 20 years after his baptism he wrote:

> "...I know that nothing good lives in me, that is, in my sinful nature. For I have the desire to do what is good, but I cannot carry it out. For what I do is not the good I want to do; no, the evil I do not want to do-- this I keep on doing. Now if I do what I do not want to do, it is no longer I who do it, but it is sin living in me that does it.
>
> So I find this law at work: When I want to do good, evil is right there with me. For in my inner being I delight in God's

law; but I see another law at work in the members of my body, waging war against the law of my mind and making me a prisoner of the law of sin at work within my members. What a wretched man I am! Who will rescue me from this body of death? Thanks be to God-- through Jesus Christ our Lord!

So then, I myself in my mind am a slave to God's law, but in the sinful nature a slave to the law of sin.

Therefore, there is now no condemnation for those who are in Christ Jesus, because through Christ Jesus the law of the Spirit of life set me free from the law of *sin and death*." - Romans 7:14-8:2

The original Greek text of the above italicized words reads differently...

There is now therefore no condemnation to them in Christ Jesus <u>who walk not after the flesh but after the spirit.</u>

Do Paul's words ring a bell with you? They sure do with me! Truth is, all Christians must deal with temptation. In fact, Christians especially come under Satan's attack. He wants to destroy us so the impact of the Gospel of Christ is limited.

It's not shame that Christians should have sin in their lives. Sin is part of our humanity, let loose by Adam and Eve. It only becomes shame when sin is left to fester and destroy what God has redeemed. Fortunately God provides us with relief. The Apostle John tells us how:

"If we claim to be without sin, we deceive ourselves and the truth is not in us. If we confess our sins, he is faithful and just and will forgive us our sins and purify us from all unrighteousness. If we claim we have not sinned, we make him out to be a liar and his word has no place in our lives." - I John 1:8-10

Mind you John is addressing Christians here. But reading this truth and actually doing something about it is where many of us fall short. There are those within our brotherhood who continue to live with unclean spirits. They may harbor fear, jealousy, worry, selfish ambition, guilt, and the like. Issues of the heart like these are of Satan, not of God. If we harbor and hold on to these unclean spirits, we separate ourselves from God, others, and even self.

For example: If we as a Christian harbor feelings of unforgiveness toward another person, how can we expect God to heal us of sickness? We cannot. We cannot because we cannot love God and harbor hatred toward another person at the same time. In doing so we separate ourselves from God's blessing.

It's not that God is unwilling or unable to heal. He is after all our healer - Psalm 103:3. It's that we must repent and desire to live sanctified before He will grant healing. Otherwise, God would be double minded. God would have to become evil in condoning evil in order to bless us in our sins.

Even as born again believers, without truth it is difficult for us to comprehend God's power to heal us from sickness. It's the same difficulty for us to comprehend that sin is behind sickness. It wasn't until sin entered the world through man, that sickness became a reality. I know it's difficult to understand, but this is only because we live in a world full of sin and sickness. Sickness in and out of the Church is now the norm. Healing is considered an oddity.

Now what I am about to say next is important for Christians to understand. Just because a Christian falls ill does not mean they have sin in their life. They may, but we should not judge them with sin without confession or consoling. That's because we live in a sinful world where bad things happen to good people. The polluted air we breathe, the processed food we eat, the water we drink, the medicines we take may all cause chronic forms of illness.

Having said that, the root cause of chronic illness is often-times the result of lack of sanctification. Healing begins when we make peace with God, ourselves and others and allow God into our hearts to work us over, what the Apostle John calls walking in the light - I John 1:7. Until those sin issues of the heart are acknowledged and given over to God for removal, there can be no health in the body.

Once we put Christ on in baptism - Romans 6:1-7, we take on a responsibility to grow in Christ (To live holy lives). God does not require our perfection to live free of sin, but he does require us to recognize fear, jealousy, worry, selfish ambition, unforgiveness, hatred, lust, and the like as sin and to repent of these things. It's unrepented sin that keeps God from healing us.

That we suffer in body should indicate the spiritual war being waged within our heart - Ephesians 6:12. To separate chronic illness from our walk with God is to deny the source of that disease (Satan), its cause (Sin) and healing (God's Peace). Healing begins when we make peace with God and allow Him in our heart to work us over. Again what the Apostle John calls walking in the light - I John 1:7.

A Spirit led man or woman understands what God has freely given them. They allow God's Spirit within to reshape their lives, their words, their thoughts, and every action. Peace, that is the Peace of Jesus Christ, dwells within their heart and soul. This is sanctification.

My son, pay attention to what I say; **listen closely to my words**. Do not let them out of your sight, keep them within your heart; for **they are life to those who find them and health to a man's whole body**. Above all else, guard your heart, for it is the well spring of life.

- Proverbs 4:20

Chapter Two

Healing the Sick in Church (The Body of Christ)

The message Jesus brought to the world was something no one had ever heard. He proclaimed the kingdom of God drawing near, and then did something most amazing. He put His words into action. Jesus healed people—as many as could get close to Him. The lesson is clear. God is breaking through to the physical world (into the affairs of man) to heal (physically and spiritually). Jesus never wavered in this teaching. He preached the Kingdom of God and healed the sick.

The more one studies the ministry of Jesus, the more one realizes the importance Jesus placed on healing the sick. For nearly one-fifth of the four Gospel accounts is devoted to Jesus' healing and the discussions raised by them. In fact, the emphasis on healing is more extensive than any other experience in the narrative.

Out of 3,779 verses in the four Gospels, 727 relate specifically to the healing of physical and mental illness and the resurrection of the dead. And the healings that are recorded represent only a small fraction of the total - John 20:30. Compare this to the 165 verses that deal in general with eternal life.

Churches who lack the wisdom of God to minister healing to the sick overlook a larger truth. It is His eternal nature and purpose to both save and heal.

> It is God's intent that through the Church the manifold wisdom of God should be made known, according to His eternal purposes, which he accomplished in Christ Jesus our Lord. In him we can approach God with freedom and confidence - Ephesians 3:10-12.

Salvation and healing are both God's wisdom and eternal purpose -Psalm 103:3-4, Isaiah 53:4-5. Many churches have forgotten this foundational, spiritual truth and are paying the price. In practical terms it means a Church (the Body of Christ) without a healing ministry is like a restaurant without a kitchen! Neither is very satisfying. Not many people show up for service, because there is nothing there to fill their hunger.

During his earthly ministry Jesus focused on two things: Proclaiming the Kingdom of God, and healing the sick of physical illness and disease. After Jesus ascended into heaven, His disciples (obeying the Great Commission) did the same as what Jesus taught them: They proclaimed the Gospel and healed the sick. That all happened here on Earth over 2,000 years ago.

So here's a question: What's changed since then?

For sake of discussion, suppose Jesus were to physically appear in our midst today. What would we do? Do you think we would crowd around Him asking Him to heal our infirmity or disease? Of course, and He would! He would heal us because of who He is, and our faith in Him. Now here's what I ask you to ponder.

Does it make any difference whether Jesus is physically here in our midst today or not to ask him for physical healing?

That's a rhetorical, gotcha question because He IS with us today. That's the whole point of the healing Gospel of Jesus Christ. **He lives within each one of us**. This explains why James exhorted Church elders to pray over the sick and anoint them with oil in the name of the Lord for healing - James 5: 14-16.

Our Personal Faith is the Key to Divine (Spiritual) Healing.

Of all the spiritual issues that confront Christians today, perhaps none is more misunderstood than the power of faith to heal the sick. Jesus said: If you have faith as tiny as a mustard seed, you can say to this mountain, move from here to there and it will move. Nothing will be impossible to you." - Matthew 17:20.

Those who do not believe in healing miracles today are quick here to point out that Jesus was addressing his disciples; that His message about faith moving a mountain was intended only for them. But, why do they say that? What verse from God's Word can they cite that backs this teaching? There is none!

To the contrary, when Jesus' disciples asked Him why they could not heal an epileptic boy, He chided them saying, "Because you have so little faith!" - Matthew 17:19-20. Could it be the same with many of us today?

Which is easier to say: "The age of miracles have ceased." Or; "Oh ye of little faith?" You see, healing miracles are all about faith; they are not bound by time or circumstance. The problem is not miracles, the problem is our lack of faith in God to heal the sick. If we have faith in God that He saves us in obeying the Gospel, what keeps our faith from believing God will heal our body when called upon through that faith? The problem is our faith (disbelief), not God's willingness to heal.

Faith in God's promise to heal is what separates men of faith in God, from carnal men who cower in fear or disbelief that God will heal them. This kind of faith is not intellectual or born of

29

doctrine: It is a soul searching conviction (born of God's Word), which touches the very heart of God.

There is perhaps no better demonstration of faith in the healing power of Jesus living in us today than the account of a crippled beggar that was healed by Peter recorded in Acts 3. Yes, Peter was an Apostle of Jesus, but that is not why the crippled man could be healed. He was healed because Peter had faith through Jesus living in him to heal the man. Remember, Peter formerly was a carnal fisherman. Peter explained...

> By faith in the name of Jesus, this man whom you see and know was made strong. It is Jesus name and the faith that comes through him that has given complete healing to him, as you all can see. - Acts 3: 16

The following point to be made is critical...Peter did not say this man was healed because he, Peter, had some special power given to Him being an Apostle of Jesus. If he had he would have said so. No, he explained **it was faith through Jesus living in Peter that transmitted healing to the crippled man**. The crippled man was only looking for money, not healing – Acts 3:3-5.

Standing the next day before the elders, rulers and high priest, Peter tied together physical healing and spiritual salvation in Christ as coming from the same source. He told them...

> Then know this, you and all the people of Israel: It is by the name of Jesus Christ of Nazareth, whom you crucified but whom God raised from the dead, that this man stands before you **healed**... **Salvation** is found in no one else, for there is no other name under heaven

given to mankind by which we must be
saved. - Acts 4:10-12 NIV

Please note: Peter made no distinction between the man's healing and salvation. We need to pay more attention to those 3 highlighted words (healed, salvation, saved). For they all 3 (used in different ways) mean the same things. In the original Greek language...

Healed means...saved, made well, in good health

Salvation means...deliverance, preservation

Saved means...preservation, healed, delivered

In using those 3 words together in context, Peter is talking about salvation from spiritually caused disease, and death. This is because for born again people with faith in God, there is no such thing as one without the other two.

1. It is by the name of Jesus this man was healed **(saved, made well)**.
2. Salvation **(preservation)** is found in no one else.
3. There is no other name by which we must be saved **(healed, preserved)**

Jerome's translation changed the word "heal" to "save."

It was Jerome who gave us the Latin Vulgate Bible. When Jerome translated the older Greek and Hebrew texts into Latin, he incorrectly translated "save" and "heal" using the same word, "salvo." In doing so he removed the physical aspects and meaning of the word "heal" by spiritualizing it.

Jerome's translation of these two words using one word was no accident. Both he and Augustine saw no need for supernatural (miracles) to continue in the Church. The result is that Jerome took liberty with older texts to suit his belief. Jerome's incorrect use of the Latin word "salvo" shows up in Acts 4:12 and James 5:15 in modern Bibles.

For instance, King James translators incorrectly interpreted "salvo" as "saved." Correctly translated from older texts, the word used should be "healed," or "made whole," not saved. Thus, Acts 4:12 and James 5:15 correctly translated should read...

> ...for there is no other name under heaven given among men, whereby by which we must be **healed.** - Acts 4:12 KJV

> ...And the prayer of faith shall **heal** the sick.
> - James 5:15 KJV

As you can see, Jerome's translation has caused extreme harm to the healing Gospel of Jesus Christ. Granted both words "heal" and "save" share similar meanings. But if they are not used in the proper context, and correctly translated from original texts, they change the logical intent and meaning of the verse into something that doesn't fit. To wit: The subject in the above verses in Acts and James is about healing the sick, not saving the sick.

When you understand what these two verses are really saying, it requires rethinking the Gospel of Jesus Christ and God's Word for what it is telling us : **God is our Healer!**

"Who Touched me?"

Another great example of how healing faith works is recorded in Mark 5:25-34. There a woman who was subject to bleeding for 12 years believed (had faith) if she could just touch Jesus' cloak she would be healed. She had been to doctors for help, but her condition only grew worse. Jesus was surrounded with people crowding against Him. Yet when the woman's hand briefly touched His garment from behind, Jesus new it instantly; because He felt power leave His body.

When Jesus asked, "Who touched me?", the woman came and fell at His feet telling Him the truth. <u>What Jesus told her in reply lives within each one of us today</u>. He said;

"Daughter, **your faith has healed you**. Go in
peace and be freed from your suffering."
- Mark 5:34

"Your faith has healed you." FAITH! How utterly wonderful and marvelous is the healing power of faith in Jesus over sickness and death.

There Are Two Kinds of Spiritual Healing:
Instantaneous, and over time.

Before beginning this section, English readers should know their ability to understand what they read is determined in part by how English words are used. For instance, If you say I love ice cream, does that mean you love ice cream as much as saying you love your family? Of course not. We just assume you love your family more than ice cream, and rightfully so.

One reason the New testament was originally penned in the Greek language is that it is very specific. In matters of

33

> importance the Greek language does not allow the reader to assume the correct meaning of a verb or noun, because assumptions are not always true or correct. For instance, The original Greek language uses 8 different words to describe the English word love (The English language uses only 1). The Greek language allows readers to fully interpret the context of the love we feel for others and objects like ice cream. English nouns and verbs by themselves, do not.

When you study the original Greek language where the English words "heal" or "healed" are used, you quickly realize <u>our English words do not allow us to fully interpret the manner of healing we read in Scripture</u>. Are you ready for this? Not every healing Jesus and the Apostles administered was instantaneous. Many, if not most of those recorded healings occurred over time. For instance:

When the Apostle Paul was marooned on the island of Patmos, he healed the father of the head official – Acts 28:8-9. That healing was instantaneous. How do we know? The original Greek word Paul used, **iaomai**, to describe the outcome is translated into English as "healed." **Iaomai** means healed instantly, or miraculously. But English readers wouldn't know that, only that he was healed. Now compare that healing to the healing that followed.

When the rest of the islanders heard about his healing, the sick came to Paul and his companions for healing. They were also healed, but Paul here uses a different word to describe their healing, because their healing was not instantaneous. The original Greek word Paul used to describe the form of their healing is **therapeuo**. It literally means to wait upon menially, to relieve of disease; yet that information is omitted in English translations. English readers only know healing occurred. They do not know how or the kind of healing that was administered. As a side note the English word therapy is derived from the Greek word **therapeuo**

When Jesus gave instructions to his 12 disciples to go out into the countryside, He told them to preach the kingdom of God and to heal (**therapeuo** – wait upon menially) the sick – Matthew 10:1, 7-8. In Mark 6:12-13 related to this event in Matthew 10, we read...They drove out many demons and anointed many sick people with oil and healed (**therapeuo**) them.

When Jesus gave instructions to 72 Disciples to go out into the countryside, He gave them this instruction: when you enter a town...heal the sick and tell them the kingdom of God is near you - Luke 10:9. The original Greek word Jesus used for heal is **therapeuo**.

As you begin to study the healings' recorded in the New Testament using a Strong's Analytical Concordance, you'll also learn the healings Jesus performed were not always the instantaneous kind. Many people Jesus healed were healed (**therapeuo**) by waiting upon them menially - Matthew 4:23-24.

So there is no doubt about the meaning or usage of these 2 words (iaomai and therapeuo), a discussion between a centurion and Jesus distinguishes the difference between the two words found in Matthew 8:5-13.

A centurion came to Jesus asking for help. He told Jesus his servant at home was paralyzed and in terrible pain. Jesus said, "I will go and heal (**therapeuo** - wait upon menially) him."

The centurion replied, "I do not deserve to have you come under my roof. But just say the word, and my servant will be healed (**iaomai** – instantly). For I myself am a man under authority, with soldiers under me. I tell this one go and he goes; and that one come, and he comes."

When Jesus heard this, He was astonished and said to those following Him. "I tell you the truth, I have not found anyone in

Israel with such great faith." Then Jesus said to the centurion, "Go! It will be done just as you believed it would." And his servant was instantly healed (**iaomai**) that very hour.

Jesus was ready to go to the centurion's house and wait upon the servant to **therapeuo** him (wait upon him menially as you or I would a loved one). But when Jesus learned of the centurion's faith in His authority, Jesus was amazed and healed (**iaomai**) the man instantly...fulfilling the centurion's faith request.

Healing Belongs to God Through Jesus Christ.

The source of all healing (both physical and spiritual) in the world emanates from God through Jesus Christ. This includes healing from a cut or bruise on your arm to major diseases like cancer or myocarditis, including death! In short, Jesus Christ has supremacy over our life.

> The Son is the image of the invisible God, the firstborn over all creation. **For in him all things were created**: things in heaven and on earth, visible and invisible, whether thrones or powers or rulers or authorities; all things have been created through him and for him. **He is before all things, and in him all things hold together**. And he is the head of the body, the church; he is the beginning and the firstborn from among the dead, so that in everything he might have the supremacy. **For God was pleased to have all his fullness dwell in him, and through him to reconcile to himself all things**, whether things on earth or things in heaven, by making

> peace through his blood, shed on the
> cross. - Colossians 1:15-20

Forgive my personal feelings here, but if reading aloud that passage doesn't make you want to get down on your knees, and shout with joy and sing praises to our Lord and Savior, what will?

Consider what "**in him all things hold together**" means. How our world spins and travels around the Earth's Sun; how the Earth spinning slowly tilts back and forth on its axis giving us 4 seasons; how our Sun's rays work in plants to make them grow; how new human life is formed and nurtured by its mother's body, how our heart beats seemingly on its own...and on and on. You get the meaning of that passage. All things were created and <u>are being actively held together</u> by and for our Lord and Savior, Jesus Christ.

Now consider what "**...to reconcile to himself all things**" means. The cut on your finger, a lump in your lungs, coronary heart disease, cancer, and every other injury or illness medical science has named...Jesus reconciles to Himself.

Said differently, without Jesus, you and I would not be here today. There are not enough words to express this truth. Praise God, Almighty!!!

Deception and Faith:

The advent of Jesus Christ, God in human flesh, is unlike any natural event before or since. While here on earth, Jesus saw Himself as being in conflict with evil. He battled Satan on a spiritual level made manifest in the physical realm. He not only paved the way for our freedom from Satan's slavery, He battled with and defeated Satan completely. This includes our healing from disease and sickness which can only originate from Satan.

What better way is there to demonstrate Christ's love for man than for Him to heal people? This is the heart and soul of what the Incarnation of Christ is about - John 3:16, and what Jesus meant when He said, "the Kingdom of God is near you" – Luke 10:9. It implies God breaking forth into the world and into the life of man to heal him from what evil has wrought.

This is the spiritual battle being fought over us between God and Satan; and why God has given us the healing Gospel of Jesus Christ (both physical and spiritual).

> ...Put on the full armor of God, so that you can take your stand against the devil's schemes. For **our struggle is not against flesh and blood, but against the rulers, against the authorities, against the powers of this dark world and against the spiritual forces of evil in the heavenly realms**. -Ephesians 6: 11-12

If Satan can get you to believe your faith is of no value to your born again body, he can limit (prevent) your faith in God to heal you, and or destroy your faith altogether. This is the spiritual war that is being fought for our souls.

Sadly, many Christians today do not recognize that sickness and disease are the result of living in a sinful world. Somewhere in time we have accepted Satan's lie that all sickness is the result of <u>natural manifestation, not spiritual manifestation</u>. And if from natural manifestation, it seems perfectly logical to go to (depend on) the world for healing. **Note:** Not all sickness and disease emanates from our sin.

If we suffer from a chronic illness, we reason the world has drugs and medical doctors to "manage" our condition. What we're not being told is medical doctors account for the 3rd leading cause of death: And prescription drugs account for the 4th leading cause of death in the USA. By contrast, You can read the New Testament from front to back, and nowhere will you read of one death caused by spiritual healing through faith in Jesus Christ.

This is not to condemn medical doctors or all modern medicine, for there certainly is a role for both to play in our lives. Where sudden, life-threatening injuries are concerned, there are pharmaceutical drugs and surgeries that save lives. Those drugs and the medical treatment given by doctors play a vital role in society, but are temporary. This Bible study is not intended to diminish their importance. Rather, our focus on the subject concerns long-term, chronic forms of disease and long-term dependence on drugs to "manage" disease.

The Role in Healing the Sick in The Body of Christ.

That our brotherhood prays to God for healing for brethren struck down with illness or injury (lifting their names to God) is most excellent and good. Those who recover from their illness or injury can know God answered prayer for healing. The cause of such illness or injury is often-times accidental from living in a world corrupted with sin. For example a fall that cracked a hip bone or rib, a car accident, or an illness brought on from an infection are three common examples. But there are also long-term illnesses (chronic forms of disease) that go unanswered in prayer to God.

That we pray for healing from these types of illnesses, yet our prayer goes unanswered should wave a red flag telling us something is amiss. This is where trained church elders and spiritually mature individuals can make a big difference in the outcome. This is why James wrote:

> Is anyone among you sick? **Let them call the elders of the church** to pray over them and anoint them with oil in the name of the Lord. And the prayer offered in faith will make the sick person well; the Lord

> will raise them up. If they have sinned,
> they will be forgiven. Therefore confess
> your sins to each other and pray for each
> other so that you may be healed. The
> prayer of a righteous person is powerful
> and effective. - James 5:14-16 (NIV)

As previously stated, chronic forms of disease are often associated with long-held sin (unclean spirits) in our life (The holder of which may not even be aware of or associate with). Without intervention to uncover the source, spiritual healing will not occur, because God will not be mocked – Galatians 6:7.

This is why God appointed elders to the Body of Christ. Unless Church elders teach this truth to brethren and make themselves available for intervention, healing will not occur. And neither will healing come from pharmaceutical drugs or medical procedures. The reason is quite simple: We have only one Healer, and He requires confession and repentance from those of us who are born again to receive His healing.

Jesus taught His disciples that sickness is often the result of holding on to evil (unclean) spirits, and that healing the body comes from removal of those spirits through a change of heart. This is why repentance and healing played such a vital role within the early Christian community. Sin and sickness both have the same spiritual root (Satan, the father of lies and our destroyer).

Certainly the Apostles taught this as they traveled and established churches. Why then does today's Church, with its so called "doctrine," so quickly dismiss the association between unclean spirits (sin) and chronic illness. Unlike their modern day counterparts, early Christians understood if a man suffers in body, he suffers in spirit and soul from unclean spirits.

The Bible says God gives every man according to his ways, and according to the fruit of his doing - Jeremiah 17:9-10. Is it such a leap in faith then to understand when unclean spirits are removed from our lives (repentance), that healing begins in our body? Why do so many churches today turn a blind eye to this truth?

An Example From My Own Life:

Many years ago, a muscle spasmed in my back. I did all the usual things one does when a muscle spasms, but to no avail.

Then one day I took the matter before God in prayer. After several minutes in quiet prayer, I heard a voice within me say, "Forget about your Mother's house."

I asked back within my heart, "Is this the reason my muscle is spasmed and will not let loose?"

"Yes," replied the voice within.

In the moment, I said, "I release the matter from my heart," my back muscle relaxed and I no longer was in pain. I thanked God for my healing and gave Him praise.

Without my consciously knowing, I carried worry over the sale of my Mother's home. A muscle spasm is how my body reacted to carrying that worry. Spiritual discernment is just one example of how God can work in our lives.

I had just experienced a healing miracle, and will tell you my life has never been the same since. It was that moment, and later with another healing miracle I witnessed that gave birth to my book, *The Miracle of Healing in Your Church Today*.

We are so far removed from what the Bible teaches about sin and sickness today. Through omission in teaching this truth, we've come to believe sin and sickness are unrelated to one another. Or at the very least we no longer believe that healing the sick is relevant in today's Church.

> Our struggle is not against flesh and blood
> but against the powers of this dark world,
> and against the spiritual forces of evil
> in the heavenly realms. - Ephesians 6:12

Unless the Body of Christ (The Church) acknowledges this spiritual fight includes our body, as well as our spirit and soul, chronic illness will forever be as much a part of Christ's Body as it is in the world.

We Mean Well, But...

Prayer is a powerful weapon against evil. But adding names to a Church prayer list and praying for them will not remove disease-caused unclean spirits, without deep and personal reflection by those afflicted. The early Church knew this. It explains why the first century Church was a healing center for the sick. The sick received individual "**therapeuo**" (healing therapy) and **"Iaomai"** (instant healing). They did this by taking captive every thought to make it obedient to Christ - 2 Corinthians 10:3-5, and through laying on of hands, anointing and prayer in ministry.

Unless Christians today afflicted with chronic illness come to grips with the truth of unclean spirits possibly being in their lives, they may never heal. They will not know the power of God to heal them. And neither will they have a testimonial to tell the world (Empty pews bear witness to this truth).

Contrast that with a Christian formerly diseased by an unclean spirit, who was healed (**therapeuo**) by God through a church healing ministry. They have a powerful healing testimony to share with the world. For those who hear their testimony, the thought of going to Church will take on a whole new dimension: Healing and salvation!

This is where healing ministries make all the difference. By asking with consent, thoughtful, confidential, personal questions about their life, a healing ministry can often isolate sin in a person's life they may not even be aware of. It's no different when one seeks spiritual counseling with an elder on other matters about family and Christian living. Elders ask questions of them. The same can be accomplished by a person afflicted checking off yes, no answers on a Spiritual and Physical Health Assessment questionnaire later reviewed by an elder or healing ministry team.

The truth is each of us must contend with unclean spirits most every day of our life. God's spiritual weapon to redeem us from unclean spirits is love — love not as the world knows it, but love as only that which comes from God, unconditional with no "ifs," "ands," or "buts." - John 3:16, I John 4:16.

The spirit of love is the exact opposite of all that evil stands for and is all powerful - I Corinthians 13. It is love that heals the body, spirit, and soul. The problem for many of us is we want His spirit called love, but often neglect to let go of certain unclean spirits that make us ill. We cannot have it both ways! James concludes his inspired word by saying,

> Remember this: Whoever turns a sinner from the error of their way will save them from death and cover over a multitude of sins. - James 5:20

The Church and Ministry:

Discernment – Separation – Sanctification

These three, discernment, separation and sanctification comprise the process to minister spiritual healing in the Church. It is not enough to teach the Gospel of salvation to the lost, we must also heal the sick. For healing (restoring, saving, to make whole) body, spirit, and soul is what the Gospel of Jesus Christ is all about.

Let me tell you a truth of God. **God receives no glory in sickness. He receives no glory in death** - Isaiah 38:18. **God receives glory in healing the sick**.

Some Christians are taught to believe being sick is a way to bring glory to God. But this kind of reasoning is completely the reverse of everything God's Word teaches us. The Gospel writer,

John, tells about a man who had been blind from birth that Jesus healed. His disciples wanted to know who caused his blindness, him or his parents? Jesus answered:

> "Neither this man nor his parents sinned," said
> Jesus, "but this happened so that **the work of**
> **God might be displayed in his life**."
> - John 9:1-3 (NIV)

What was the work of God in this man's life? Jesus healed the man of his blindness. Praise God. Healing is the work of God. Healing is His glory. It wasn't the man's blindness that brought glory to God. It was his healing that brought glory to God. Had the man's blindness been for the glory of God, does anyone honestly believe Jesus would have healed the man?

Again, God receives glory in healing, not sickness. Why then does the Body of Christ (the Church) today seem so content to NOT minister healing to the sick? Not healing the sick violates everything Jesus suffered in body and died for - Isaiah 53:4-5.

This is why the Church was given a five-fold ministry.

> It was he who gave some to be apostles, some to be prophets, some to be evangelists, and some to be pastors and teachers, to prepare God's people for works of service, so that the body of Christ may be built up until we all reach unity in the faith and in the knowledge of the Son of God and become mature, **attaining to the whole measure of the fullness of Christ.** – Ephesians 4: 11-13 (NIV)

"Attaining to the whole measure of the fullness of Christ" is inclusive of every aspect of our being, body, spirit and soul:

For we ARE members of His Body. There is a lesson here for evangelists, pastors, and teachers in the Church.

Today many churches have individuals written down on their sick lists. Let me ask: How do you feel knowing many on those lists could die before their time? - Psalm 139:16.

God said, "Man's days will be 120 years" – Genesis 6:3. Some Bible scholars say that was God's declaration the great flood would occur 120 years from His pronouncement. Other scholars disagree with that interpretation. One thing certain: Here in the USA the average life expectancy is 73.4 years. In Singapore and Switzerland the average life expectancy is 84 years. Only a very few people ever reach the age of 120 years! Those statistics should tell you something. Satan is taking our brethren to an early grave, hindering God to spread the Good News of Jesus Christ. The net result is we, God's people, have overlooked the cost of sin, its affect on our longevity, evangelism, congregational worship and fellowship.

I believe our heart is in the right place to minister to the sick. I only ask these questions to point out: We know something is amiss within the Body when so many of our number are sick and dying from disease, instead of old age.

Sin within the Body of Christ is a major problem, exactly because we do not like to talk about it. Neither are we prepared to deal with it in many cases. We don't know how to reach out to those in need for healing. Prayer for healing often goes unanswered because those with chronic disease often (not always) have spiritual issues with their old man of sin they have NOT dealt with.

The bottom line is that many of our sick in Christ are in need of spiritual, physical healing **so the life of Jesus may be revealed in their body** - II Corinthians 4:11. So I ask: If not healing from the Church (the Body of Christ), from whom? If not now, when?

No medical doctor or psychologist is prepared to deal with the issues of sin and holiness responsible for physical and spiritual sickness. This is why after spending 2 trillion dollars and over

700,000 physicians, over 2 million people in the health field; out of all our hospitals, medications and procedures, the medical community has failed to heal even one person of a single chronic disease.

This is why God gave us the Church, the Body of Christ: To minister to the body, spirit, and soul of people living with sin and sickness. Share this study with your Church. Encourage Church leaders to look past what they think they know about spiritual healing in the Church, and get back into The Word. Join me in prayer that hearts will open to receive this truth. Thank you and many blessings.

Chapter Three

Christians, Witchcraft and Drugs

What would you think if the next time you take the Lord's Supper a drug is offered to you instead of bread? "Crazy," you say?

No faithful Christian would knowingly replace bread (which represents the Body of Jesus) with a drug (pill). And yet, this is what is happening millions of times everyday. Many Christians routinely taking drugs forget the sacrifice Jesus made in body on their behalf for healing.

Keep your eyes on the pill:

What is it about man's fascination with drugs that holds such sway over the Body of Christ? Why do so many Christians trust a pill over God with their body? Well, a lot of it has to do with the original King James (KJ) Bible translators.

During the time when the KJ Bible was first being translated, witches and witchcraft occupied the minds of many Church leaders. Hundreds of people were tried and executed for being a witch. So when KJ Bible translators came to the Greek word "**pharmakeia**" in the New Testament, they choose to use the lesser meaning of the word, "witchcraft, sorcery" instead of the word's primary meaning, "**use of drugs**."

At the time of translation back in 1611, using the word "witchcraft" must have made sense. Witches created and used drugs and potions made from plants, animal innards and chemicals. So the word, witchcraft, fit the times and translators wanted to make that point. After all, God condemns witchcraft, "**kesheph**," found in II Kings 9:22

That's all well and good except that: When we read about the "acts of the flesh" in Galatians 5:19-21 today, no mention is made of using drugs, only of witchcraft. Here's how KJ translators translated the passage:

> Now the works of the flesh are manifest, which are these; Adultery, fornication, uncleanness, lasciviousness, Idolatry, **witchcraft,** hatred, variance, emulations, wrath, strife, sedition, heresies, Envying, murders, drunkenness, revelings, and such like: of the which I tell you before, as I have also told you in time past, that they which do such things shall not inherit the kingdom of God.
> - Galatians 5:19-21 **King James Bible**

Now compare that same passage correctly translated from the Greek text using the Heritage Bible and notice how different it reads:

> And the works of the flesh are manifest, which are: Adultery, sexual promiscuity, uncleanness, lack of moral restraint, Idolatry, **use of drugs**, hatred, quarreling, jealousies, hard breathing,

> strife, dissensions, heresies, Envyings,
> murders, drunkenness, carousings, and
> the such like, which I tell you before, as I
> also said previously, that those practicing
> such things will absolutely not inherit
> the kingdom of God.
> - Galatians 5:19-21 **Heritage Bible**

There it is: "Use of drugs." There is absolutely nothing mentioned about witchcraft, because the primary Greek word meaning of pharmakeia means use of drugs. It's not until you get into a secondary meaning where you then will find witchcraft and sorcery.

"Houston, we have a problem."

Christians today are faced with the same problem KJ Bible translators had back in 1611, only in reverse. Witchcraft is not the issue of the day, pharmaceutical drugs are.

The medical, industrial and agricultural drug industry today dominates our lives. Drug use is so prevalent, drug traces show up in our food and water supply, and even threatens extinction of certain plants, animals and marine life. But that problem only touches the hem of the garment. The real problem lies in the human death toll created directly through legally prescribed drug consumption.

Witches do not cause this problem. The problem is caused by a giant industry that wants every man, woman and child hooked on their product: Drugs! In fact, the Bible warns of this very thing happening: Here is how the Heritage Bible interprets the Book of Revelation with the Greek word pharmakeia.

> And the light of a lamp will absolutely
> not shine in you any more, and the voice
> of the bride-groom and of the bride will

49

> absolutely not be heard in you any more, because **your merchants** were the great ones of the earth, because **in your spell inducing drugs** (pharmakeia) **all the races were led astray**.
>
> - Rev. 18:23 Heritage Bible

Pharmakeia in Luke's, John's and Paul's language of Koine Greek literally means "medication from a pharmacy," (what were then called sorcerers). In fact, it is from "pharmakeia" that we get our English words pharmacy, pharmacist and pharmacology.

God condemns "pharmakeia" because it is of "the works of the flesh," in opposition to "the fruits of the Spirit." This truth in today's world is hard for many Christians to believe and accept.

God's Word lists pharmakeia as a work of the flesh, because those who turn to pharmaceutical drugs (and those who encourage their use) place dependency on a false reality (an illusion) instead of in God our Healer - Exodus 15:26.

The Truth About Pharmaceutical Drugs

A report by the General Accounting Office in the United States revealed that 51.5% of all drugs introduced between 1976 and 1985 had to be re-labeled because of serious adverse reactions found after the marketing of these drugs. Those "side effects" included heart, liver and kidney failure, fetal toxicity and birth defects, severe blood disorders, respiratory arrest, seizures, and blindness. The changes to the labeling either restricted a drug's use or added major warnings. Still, the carnage continues unabated. (Source: FDA Drug Review: *Post Approval Risks 1976-1985*, US General Accounting Office, April 1990)

Pharmaceutical drugs never heal disease. Rather, they kill and maim millions of people every year. In a June 2010 report in the Journal of General Internal Medicine: Authors stated in looking over records that spanned from 1976 to 2006, they found that of 62 million death certificates, 25 million deaths were coded as having occurred in a hospital setting due to **medication errors**. The total number of deaths due to the American modern medical system of drugging, unnecessary surgeries, infections, medical errors, etc., is nearly 800,000 people per year!

The pharmaceutical industry today has become so powerful, it literally owns (controls) governments, including United States bureaucracies. Millions of dollars are handed out to medical doctors and agencies who through bribery carry out its demands. See Matthew 7:20.

With such a record, the pharmaceutical industry would be considered criminal by any other civilized standard. However, it is condoned by law, medicine, and the uninformed in the U.S.A. And for what? In spite of heavy promotion, **there has never been a pharmaceutical drug that has healed a single disease**. No man-made chemical drug ever will. Drugs can only mask, cover-up, or eliminate symptoms. Not heal.

Are Christians Condemned for Taking "Medication From a Pharmacy?"

In a word, no!

God's grace is greater than our sin. Read a little further down in Galatians 5:21 "...those who **LIVE** like this will not inherit the kingdom of heaven." That word, "live," means to perform routinely or habitually. So, God's Word is referring here to continual, regular drug use.

Does this make short-term use of drugs okay?

Drugs are not a black and white issue. Drugs can be useful to kill pain, and stop infection. There are circumstances where drugs are used only short-term, and then very carefully monitored. This report is not directed against their use in this circumstance. But all drugs are spiritually dangerous, i.e. like those we see advertised in television commercials.

God never intended that we should spend half our income on drugs to maintain our lives. Drugs, by their very nature, only mask and cover-up health problems. They cannot heal.

Fortunately, we are blessed to have many different kinds of medicine in our culture from which to choose. No one is forcing us to submit to pharmakeia as our only choice. That is a ruse on the part of the pharmaceutical industry.

The problem is most people today only know to go to an allopathic physician when they fall sick. They know their doctor is going to prescribe drugs to them. What they don't know is drugs are the ONLY treatment their doctor is trained and allowed to prescribe when allopathic protocol calls for their use.

I am not speaking against allopathic doctors here. The diagnostic machines and tests available to doctors provide them with very precise (in most cases) diagnosis. They perform a great service in this department.

What I am trying to point out is...

The way our system works through health insurance programs (which cater almost exclusively to allopathic physicians) and massive TV advertising of allopathic medicine (pharmakeia), people have come to believe and place their hope and trust in that system alone.

Other legitimate forms of medicine, through politics, insurance plans and money, have been largely sidelined from public exposure. These include: Homeopathic medicine, Chiropractic medicine, Osteopathic medicine, Acupuncture, Reflexology, Holistic medicine, Chinese medicine and Ayurveda medicine to name but a few.

I know this whole topic of divine healing, healing oil, anointing and pharmakeia is scary stuff for most everyone. It forces us to re-examine our faith (Something we do NOT like to do). We like being comfortable where we are, because it's our nature not to step out of our comfort zone.

So when someone comes along and speaks as I have, the first tendency it has is to tighten the screws on our faith. We think there is something here to fear because the teaching is new. It is as though we have God sewed up in a bag, and we do not want anyone loosing the tie string at the top to let Him out.

Fortunately, there has never been a more promising time for good medicine to heal us. More and more integrated healing facilities are opening up which practice holistic medicine. I believe holistic medicine will continue to gain favor with the public, because this form of medicine works to heal (with great success) without harming the body or mind.

The Church (The Body of Christ) Then and Now...

I know this information is alarming to many, especially those whose lives (they believe) are dependent on drugs. **But the truth is the early Church never separated sin from sickness and disease**. Neither did this teaching end with the passing of the last Apostle. It continued on for hundreds of years. The early church was where people went for both physical and spiritual healing in their lives (Read James 5:13-20). Early Church elders understood the source and association between sin and sickness.

Today, however, not so much. The Church today is but a shadow of its former self, due largely to the unclean spirit that whispered in the ear of man that God is out of the healing business. It is a lie from the father of lies. **Chronic sickness and disease today is accepted both in and out of the Church as being the result of natural manifestation, not a spiritual manifestation.** Nothing could be further from the truth.

For a generation of Christians who grew up with drug proliferation and a trusted medical industry that heavily pushes them, drugs seem normal and acceptable. Our generation of Christians believes the big lie that "drugs are good for you." You

53

could even say, the pharmaceutical industry has won us over from our faith in God that He is our healer.

Many Christians today think pharmaceutical prescription drugs are different from illegal drugs because they are used by the AMA medical system and regulated by the FDA. They trust anyone wearing a white rob to prescribe and dispense drugs. They do so without understanding that **most everything about the pharmaceutical industry violates the spiritual foundational truth and teaching of God.**

That's not to say we shouldn't seek medical help from a physician. The problem, however, is most physicians are secular and know only pharmakeia, surgery, chemotherapy and radiation. They are not taught about Yahweh-Rapha, or the healing provision He placed in the plant kingdom for our health and well-being. But in most cases it's not the physician's fault. Physicians only know (and are required) to treat patients according to the allopathic modality they were taught.

Because the Body of Christ fails to teach God's natural laws and the healing power found in the Body of Jesus Christ, millions of Christians have turned to the world for healing. It's sad, but they may be doing so without God.

Without an accurate translation of God's Word to guide them on the subject, millions of God-loving people have been led astray. They have been seduced by the world to rely on drugs instead of relying on God's natural law (found in the Bible) and the Body of Jesus Christ for healing. Without knowing the truth or why, many Christians have replaced the bread of the Lord's Supper (representing healing and health through the Body of Jesus) with reliance on drugs for healing and health.

Imagine how different our faith would be today had the KJ Bible translated pharmakeia as "use of drugs" instead of "witchcraft." Almost all of Christendom knows and uses the KJ Bible. Some regard the KJ Bible as the only authorized translation and use no other Bible. So how are these people to know God condemns the practice of routinely using pharmaceutical drugs? They will not.

The truth is: God is our healer! That declaration removes all other possibilities. God has provided for our every need found in the plant kingdom and through Jesus Christ. Those who look elsewhere will find only suffering and death.

If this truth leaves you struggling, you have been victimized by the prince of this world. My prayer is that you turn away from the false reality of drugs, and turn to God's Word for truth and healing.

Chapter Four

The Working of Nature and Miracles

What is a miracle? Do miracles happen today? Some people look upon a newborn baby and proclaim this new being to be a miracle. Others would argue that new life is simply an operation of the law of nature. What is the truth behind miracles?

Part of the problem we have being able to understand a miracle is our own fallibility. We are predisposed to evil - Romans 3:23. We struggle with greed, selfish ambition, hatred, lust, jealousy, pride, etc. - Galatians 5:19. We tend to fear retribution and ridicule from other men were we to think differently from them. Though our hearts be lifted up toward God in faith, we still see the world around us; and so, we often surrender to its reality. Our faith falters and we are brought down.

A biblical example of this is when Jesus asked Peter to step out of the boat and come to Him on the water - Matthew 14:25ff. Preachers like to say, "It wasn't until Peter took his eyes off Jesus that Peter begin to sink into the waves. The wind and waves represent the world, and the world was Peter's reality. His faith in Jesus was replaced with fear of the natural world." That is all very true.

The episode with Peter was recorded in Scripture to illustrate our own frailty, fallibility, and lack of faith. No human can walk on water, we say. Neither can humans fly through the air without the aid of a machine. But Jesus, the son of man, the Son of God, did both. Was it Jesus' faith as the son of man that enabled him to walk on water, to fly up in the clouds, or was it Jesus' faith as the Son of God?

Of all the spiritual issues that confront Christians, perhaps none is more misunderstood than the power of faith to perform miracles. Jesus said: If you have faith as tiny as a mustard seed, you can say to this mountain, "Move from here to there' and it will move. Nothing will be impossible to you" - Matthew 17:20.

Again, which is easier to say: "The age of miracles have ceased." Or; "Oh ye of little faith?" You see, miracles are all about faith; they are not bound by time or circumstance. The problem is not miracles. The problem is our lack of faith to believe in miracles.

As a member of the The Body of Christ who believes in and witnessed healing miracles, I have had every argument there is explained to me why the age of miracles have ceased. Scholarly presentations were made and debated. My heart goes out to my brothers who defend against miracles; because for many years I, myself, taught against belief that miracles happen today. I know well the struggles my heart went through as I wrestled with the Scriptures and Church doctrine. It is no different for anyone else.

And no, I do not believe my faith will move a mountain. My faith has yet to grow to the size of a mustard seed (but I'm working on it). I now believe the reason Jesus measured the amount of faith required to move a mountain is to illustrate how little our faith really is.

By comparison, look at God's faith. It was through His faith the world and universe were created. - Hebrews 11:3. Here is one of the first acts and articles of faith, which is common to all believers in every age: Being sure of what we hope for and certain of what we do not see – Hebrews 11:1.

Critics will say, no, it is by OUR faith that we believe God framed the world by His commands. I beg to differ. Certainly God commanded, but He did so through faith His Word would be carried out. The biblical definition of faith demands it - Hebrews 11:1.

The Argument Against Miracles Today

The argument that miracles have ceased originates with two men who have had profound influence on modern day theology, Martin Luther and John Calvin.

Luther concluded the day of miracles is past, and the real gift of the Holy Spirit is to enlighten Scripture. He wrote, "Now that the Apostles have preached the Word and have given their writings, and nothing more than what they have written remains to be revealed, no new and special revelation or miracle is necessary." *(Sermons on the Gospel of St. John, Chapters 14-16, Luther's Works, 24:367)*

John Calvin would write: "The gift of healing disappeared with the other miraculous powers which the Lord was pleased to give for a time, that it might render the new preaching of the Gospel for ever wonderful. Therefore, even were we to grant that anointing was a sacrament of those powers, which were then administered by the hands of the Apostles; it pertains not to us, to whom no such powers have been committed. *(John Calvin, Institutes Of The Christian Religion IV.18 (1953), 2:636)*

In today's world of theological academia, I Corinthians 13:8-13 is frequently referenced to support the views held by Luther and Calvin. But there is nothing in those verses that says God will end healing miracles. If there is, I beg someone to tell me where it is. Luther may have well been reacting to the excesses of the medieval Church when he penned those words. No one knows for sure.

What we do know is that both Luther and Calvin's theology lives on today in many Christian denominations. Their impact on religious beliefs is profound. The best biblical argument opponents have to dispel belief in miracles today remains I Corinthians 13:8-10. It reads:

> "Love never fails. But where there are prophecies, they will cease; where there are tongues, they will be stilled; where there is knowledge, it will pass away. For we know in part and we prophesy in part, but when **perfection** comes, the imperfect disappears."

Those opposing miracles argue "perfection" refers to the New Testament. Thus, they conclude the need for miracles (i.e. healing miracles) is no longer required, since the New Testament is now completed.

Healing miracles, they say, were allowed by God only to: 1) Help Jesus prove his Deity and authority over all things, and: 2) Help the Disciples to prove their message was from God. Once these two things had been accomplished and the Word of God was completed, miracles ceased. The problem is: **There is no mention healing miracles will cease in their proof text.** To the contrary: Read John 14:12-13.

This opposition dogma is badly flawed for three reasons:

1. **It uses a bad hermeneutic.**

The only way I Corinthians 13:8-10 can fit as a proof text for opposition to miracles is through the use of inference. Inference can be a good thing when used properly. But used here, to infer the word "perfection" refers to the New Testament, creates conflict with the context of both Chapter 12 and 13. It's forcing a square peg to fit into a round hole.

Granted Paul does not plainly state what "perfection" is, so we must rely on inference if we are to understand his meaning. However, only when we properly understand Verses 8-10, in context with the previous Chapter 12 and all of Chapter 13, can we make a reasonable inference.

Many Christians, including myself, believe the perfection Paul refers to in Verse 10 is **love demonstrated in the return of Jesus Christ** (See verse 12 below).

> "Now we see but a poor reflection as in a
> mirror; then we shall see face to face."

Verse 12 is explained in many ways, but here's my take on it. We are created in the image of God, in His likeness. Jesus is God Incarnate (God in the flesh), but Jesus is not here. He is in heaven. When we look into a mirror, the image we see is our own face. That image is a reflection of the human face of Jesus Christ. When Christ returns, we will see him face to face. At that time there will be no further need for God to impart spiritual gifts, for those of us in Christ will be with God.

Notice also how Paul summarizes his discourse in verse 13: "And now these three remain, faith, hope and love. But the greatest of these is love." Why, because all three are the hallmarks of our heavenly Father. And notice that faith, a requirement of miracles, is one of the three hallmarks.

2. It confuses the gift of healing with gifts of healing.

Just as some Christians confuse the gift of the Holy Spirit with the gifts of the Spirit, so too does opposition dogma confuse the gift of healing with gifts of healing. Opponents argue the gifts of healing have ended, along with speaking in tongues and prophecies. But in doing so, they also lump in the gift of healing.

Gifts are spiritual attributes appointed to specific Christians in order to build, strengthen and edify the Church - I Corinthians 12:27-31. But the gift of the Holy Spirit and the gift of healing are different. They are freely available to all mankind through all ages. Just as God provides every believer with His gift of the Holy Spirit, so too, does he provide us with His gift of healing.

As previously stated, God is our healer - Exodus 15:26. The Hebrew word used here is Yahweh-Rapha, and means "the God who heals you." Think of those words carefully. Where does healing, be it physical or spiritual, originate? It originates with God! Now, ask yourself why this is so? The answer lies in understanding the answer to the next question: Who is our destroyer?

Throughout God's Word one grand theme emerges:
GOD HEALS!

Someone asks, "I thought the main theme of the Bible is "Jesus Saves." Certainly, Jesus saves: But, saying so is like saying Charles Lindbergh flew airplanes—it leaves out a big part of his story. Healing (restoring man to wholeness) has always been uppermost in God's mind – Psalm 103:3-4.

From the foundation of creation, God had a plan to restore man back to health, in body, in spirit, and soul, to free man of spiritual unclean spirits. The Bible records God's divine remedy for doing exactly that.

However, for many Christians God's Word is a book of salvation, not a book of wholeness or healing. It is this limiting view of God's Word that has opened the door for unclean (evil) spirits to plague Christian bodies and minds with chronic illness.

Also, many Christians do not look upon disease as being the result of an unclean spirit. So they reason: Sickness and disease are simply the result of natural manifestation. Why should the Church concern itself with healing the sick other than to show compassion?

This reasoning is carried over from the old agnostic teaching that teaches all human flesh is inherently evil; that the human spirit will eventually be freed of the body in death. Agnostics did not believe in the physical resurrection of the body from the grave - I Corinthians 15:12-19.

God created man to be body, spirit, and soul - Genesis 2:7. Without all three elements dwelling together, we are incomplete as human beings. We are not whole. So any attack on one part of man is an attack on the whole of man.

This is the reason why God is as equally interested in our human body and spirit as He is in our soul. For God not only considers our soul to be holy, but our spirit and body as well. His great work of restoration is able to make and keep us whole and holy, both now and for eternity.

3. It overlooks miracles today.

What if someone witnesses a healing miracle and others disbelieve the healing is miraculous? Does their disbelief cancel out or make the healing less a miracle? No, of course not. It only means there are those who do not believe in miracles. I can tell you of healing miracles, which others will dismiss as miracles. They will say those healings happened through divine providence, and do it with conviction in their hearts. They will not consider the possibility that a miracle really did occur. I can speak as I do about the matter because I once made those same claims with the same air of confidence. I was proud of "rightfully dividing" God's Word, and contended openly with those who believed differently.

Though Christians (who do not believe in miracles today) will not admit to it, in the innermost secret place of their heart, there is longing for miracles to be real. That's because we are spiritual beings: In body, in spirit, and soul. Even the most ardent disbeliever of miracles will pray to God for healing when the life of a loved one is at stake.

In my book, *"The Miracle of Healing In Your Church Today,"* I tell the story of Debbie. Debbie refused to accept the "your husband is not expected to live" death sentence handed to her by a doctor.

The doctor told Debbie, "We believe we have diagnosed your husband's blood disease, and it is called TTP (Thrombotic Thrombocytopenici Purpura). We don't expect your husband to live through the night!"

But Debbie had just spoken to the Lord. She had received God's Word that Pete would survive, and her faith was strong. She replied, "Oh don't worry about it. The Lord just spoke to me in the chapel and told me he was going to heal my husband."

The doctor looked back at her as if to say she had lost her mind and said, "No, I don't think you understand what I'm saying. We don't expect him to live through the night."

With her face aglow in faith, and without hesitation, Debbie fired back, "No, you don't understand what I'm saying. The Lord is going to heal Pete."

Bravo, for Debbie's faith, what a heroine! It should come as no surprise that Pete did not die that night but experienced a sudden and unexplained recovery. Praise the Lord! Was Pete's healing the providence of God or a miracle? Should you ask Pete's doctor, what would he say? What would Debbie say?

Providence and Miracles

What is God's providence? How is providence different from a miracle, if it is different? Must a miracle suspend natural law to be called a miracle?

The answers to those questions may surprise you and be more subjective than you would like them to be. They may also be more of a mouthful than you can comfortably chew, spiritually speaking. So chew on what you can and leave the rest for another time. Now let's go to God's Word for insight. Paul wrote:

> "...for in him (Jesus Christ) were all things created, in the heavens and upon the earth, things visible and things invisible, whether thrones or dominions or principalities or powers; all things have been created through him, and unto him; and he is before all things, **and in him all things consist**."
>
> - Colossians 1:16-17 (ASV)

The words in bold letters in the verse above means: In him all things **hold together**. There is an active, dynamic component expressed in those two words many overlook. I believe Verse 17 means **you and I, and everything in the universe, exist and function through the active, dynamic power of Jesus Christ expressed through faith. Nothing and no one can exist or live without Jesus' faith at work. All things and beings are sustained, live and die through His faith.**

Now let me give you a working example of what I mean. What makes a kernel of corn germinate and grow? Is it moisture, sunlight and earth? No, these elements only represent the environment in which corn requires to grow. A kernel of corn germinates because Jesus Christ sustains it to germinate and grow through faith - Colossians 1:17.

The world, however, sees only the three elements needed for corn to grow. The world does not see the Son of God sustaining all things through faith. But...

The world and its natural laws were not created to function apart unto themselves. Rather, **natural laws are governed directly by and through the active faith of Jesus Christ. He**

64

is the mastermind (through His faith), the regulator, and the power that gives birth to life and death to all creation.

Does not this spiritual understanding make all of life a miracle? That a kernel of corn should germinate; that a mountain should move; or a man walks on water happens through faith. It does not mean that natural law is suspended or arrested. It means God, through Jesus Christ, is **directly enabling (directing) natural law (all of life) through faith.**

The idea that God created the universe and left it to operate on its own accord to function through natural law is, in my opinion, unscriptural. But this is how many people view divine providence. They believe divine providence is God revisiting natural law and working within its laws to affect an outcome.

To say that it is not miraculous intervention for God to work within His own laws to affect a certain outcome, does not consider the action of faith required to "hold all things together." If that kind of faith in action is not miraculous, nothing is.

Conclusion:

Remember I said at the top of this chapter that we are prone to fear the world? I believe Christians, who call miraculous events "divine providence," do so in part, because divine providence is an acceptable term to the world. Divine providence is explainable, miracles are not. The world accepts God working through natural law to effect an outcome (i.e. a television documentary explained how the Red Sea could part from an erupting volcano hundreds of miles away that occurred at the time Moses raised his staff). But the world will not accept God transcending or overriding natural law.

Christians who proclaim healing miracles are subject to ridicule and scrutiny, both from within and outside the Church. So the question is asked again: Which is easier to say, "The age of miracles have ceased." Or; "Oh ye of little faith?"

Chapter Five

Healing Through Natural Law

> His divine power has given us everything
> we need for life and godliness through
> our knowledge of Him who called us
> — II Peter 1:3

When God created the world, He placed into the plant kingdom everything we would need to nurture and keep our body running at optimum health.

> Then God said, I give you every seed-
> bearing plant on the face of the whole
> earth and every tree that has fruit with
> seed in it. They will be yours for food.
> - Genesis 1:29

The word "food" in Genesis 1:29-30 carries with it a much deeper meaning than satisfying hunger. The Hebrew Word here means "Meat." The intent of which is to convey well-being, health, and needed essentials to sustain life.

When we eat, we mostly do so to satisfy hunger. We do this without giving any thought to the 30 trillion cells that make up our fleshly body or their needs. Our cells could care less about our hunger. They live or die by the water and nutrients (what we call food) we may digest. So long as Adam and Eve ate food from the Garden, there was no thought of sickness or need for healing.

However, sickness and suffering quickly became the issue of the day when Adam and Eve were removed from the Garden. If man were to survive, he would have to have access to medicine. He would have to know which plants were for food and which were for healing or for both. What's the most likely answer to how man learned about plants for healing?

During the Patriarchal Age, God spoke directly to the patriarchs. We are not privy to what all God spoke to these men, but logic and common sense dictates He pointed them to plants that have healing qualities. He would also have given Patriarch's instruction on how to use these plants. How do I know this? Common sense, again. Since we know God spoke to Patriarch's, it is logical to assume this is how man's earliest knowledge of medicine was learned.

The secular world would have you believe man arose from the apes, that man learned through trail and error what plants were good for ailments. But consider this: There wasn't time for trial and error to set the standard. Without an effective medicine, mankind could not have survived.

One thing for certain: From earliest recorded history, mankind has desired and sought out plants that heal. So much so, commerce quickly grew up around the trading of these plants and the products they produced. In Genesis 37:25 we read:

> Then they sat down to eat a meal. And as they raised their eyes and looked, behold, **a caravan of Ishmaelites** was coming from Gilead, with their camels **bearing aromatic gum and balm and**

**myrrh, on their way to bring them
down to Egypt.** – Genesis 37:25 (NAS)

Gum, balm and myrrh were highly valued as medicine, and used as trading commodities. This is why the trading caravan was headed to Egypt. When the sons of Israel prepared to return to Egypt with their younger brother Benjamin, Israel told them:

> If it must be so, then do this: **take some of the best products of the land** in your bags, and carry down to the man as a present, **a little balm and a little honey, aromatic gum and myrrh, pistachio nuts and almonds.** -Genesis 43:11 (NAS)

Here we learn that balm, honey, gum and myrrh were the best products of the land. Why? They were known for their healing qualities and highly sought after.

Application:

Something we need to relearn. No man can improve on the medicine God provided and placed into the plant kingdom. He did this so each and every generation would have access to healing remedies.

No one has ever created a drug or medicine that equals what God created. Every time someone discovers a healing element in a plant and then synthesizes that element in the form of a chemical drug, it fails. It fails because natural elements only work with other natural elements. Drugs are not natural to the human natural body.

Once you put two and two together, it becomes obvious. God created us. He knows how our bodies work and what they require to maintain optimum health. When our body becomes ill with sickness, who knows better than our creator what we need to restore our body back to health? No one. So it should not be a surprise to anyone that when God created the plant kingdom, He created a medicine chest. He placed into the plant kingdom the exact medicine for every ailment every generation needs.

For instance there are plants that are anti-viral, anti-bacterial, anti-cancerous; plants that lower blood pressure, dissolve blood clots and on and on...If modern man only knew them.

Here are just a few examples of what plants heal and keep us healthy. There are too many to list all of them here.

Lemon oil rubbed on the wrist reduces high blood pressure.
Pine needle tea (shikimmic acid) dissolves blood clots.
Apricot and apple seeds (vitamin B17) destroy cancer cells.
Apple cider vinegar with the mother restores pH balance.
Turmeric Curcumin relieves joint pain and inflammation.
Lavender oil applied to cuts and burns alleviates scarring and infection.

How Plant Oils Stopped the Bubonic Plague (Black death) in the 1400's

When the Bubonic plague struck England in 1348, mass panic set in. it was so bad, no one would come near a corpse. Corpses were often left where they were found. No one wanted to touch them. At the time no one knew it was rats that carried infected fleas as the cause. Rats were common on ships that carried trade goods, and that's how the plague came to England.

After a time, people began noticing a band of thieves (4 men) who would routinely touch and rob the dead of valuables, without becoming infected. This went on for sometime. When the King of England heard of this, he had the men rounded up and brought before him. The king wanted to know how they seemingly were immune to the plague. After striking a deal with the king to spare their lives, they told him their secret.

It turns out these men were what at the time called perfumers (today called aromatherapists). As perfumers they also were traders who traveled the Silk Road. Their knowledge of plant oils and spices taught them the exact oils to apply on their bodies to protect themselves from the plague.

These 4 men formulated (combined together) five plant oils, to give themselves the shield needed to guard against infection while robbing infected bodies. The five plant oils were cinnamon, clove, eucalyptus, lemon, and rosemary. Each of these five plants produces oil with different healing properties. When blended together, the mixture can produce the most amazing qualities.

Mind you, these men were not playing Russian Roulette with their lives. They must have already known the power of these five plant oils, or they would have never touched the dead. Understandably, the call then went out to purchase as many of these plant oils as humanly possible to end the plague.

As a side note: Those 5 plant oils have since been distilled and formulated into an essential oil blend called...Ready for it? Thieves!

Understand early man lived much closer to the Earth than we do today. Our early ancestors knew which plants were used for specific purposes. When it comes to natural health and eating today however, we only know what tastes good, its cost, and where to go to find it. When we become sickly, we go to MD's who prescribe toxic pharmaceutical drugs to us. In other words, when it comes to health and eating, a large disconnect exists between how we think and treat our physical body as it relates to our Lord, Jesus Christ's body.

Plant oils match our body's biological requirements for healing.

Plant oils (essential oils) are to plants what blood is to animals and humans. They not only sustain life in plants, they (by design) contain biological chemical constituents compatible with and essential to sustaining human life as well. In other words those chemical elements enable our bodies to do such things as grow and repair tissue, to feed our bodies essential nutrients required to sustain life. This includes the ability of our bodies to overcome infections, wounds, and disease, which is exactly what our Creator had in mind when He created the plant kingdom. And so it is, by the very nature of essential oils being the life-blood of the plant kingdom, they also match our body's biological requirements for nutrition and healing...Read on.

Plants require many of the very same elements humans require to remain strong and healthy. No wonder plants are so beneficial to the human body. By paralleling the biological requirements of our own body in plants, God has created the perfect source for our health and well-being — a virtual nutritional, medicinal cabinet lying at our feet, perfectly suited for animal and human beings alike.

The perfection of this nutritional medicinal cabinet lies in how well our own body interacts with these substances. Whether eating plants for nutrition, or utilizing them for disease prevention and healing, the liquid that flows through stems and leaves (the plant's lifeblood) closely matches that of our own life-giving blood. For just as our own blood cleanses, protects, oxygenates, nourishes, and heals, so too, do the natural oils found in plants. Plant oils contain amino acid precursors, coenzyme A factors, trace minerals, enzymes, oxygenating molecules, vitamins, and more. This is the reason why healing oils have come to be known as essential oils.

Essential oils are many times more therapeutically potent than the plant or herb from which they are derived. This is because essential oils are volatile. They vaporize when exposed to air. When a plant is cut and dried, the life-giving oil that gives the plant its therapeutic value vaporizes leaving only a dried plant. In fact, dry herbs contain only about 10% of their original oil. Because essential oils are distilled from living plants and bottled, their therapeutic value becomes concentrated and more potent than the plant or herb by itself.

When applied on the skin, inhaled, or consumed internally, essential oils work synergistically with the body, helping to maintain, repair, and renew virtually every biological organ and function, right down to DNA structure. Even more remarkably, essential oils, as food, repel and prevent life-threatening pathogens from infesting the body. More on this in a few paragraphs.

Unlike man-made antibiotics and drugs, whose function is single-phase, the natural chemical molecules of essential oils are multiple-phase. That is to say, they are not limited to one function. Further, unlike antibiotics, which can move only as our blood carries them along, essential oils are omni-directional, not being limited in direction of movement. This means essential oils can find microbes in hiding that antibiotics would otherwise pass by. Because of their chemical composition, essential oils can penetrate human and animal cell membranes, transporting oxygen and nutrients, which antibiotics cannot.

Because essential oils are volatile, their airborne chemical molecules are able to influence our emotional and spiritual state of mind. **They stimulate emotional release and spiritual cleansing**. Research has shown that the effect of such compounds, when inhaled, can exert a strong influence on the hypothalamus (the hormone command center) and limbic system (the seat of emotions) of the body. The ability of essential oils to act on both the mind and body is what makes them truly unique among natural therapeutic agents.

In every way, essential oils are God's perfect match to meet our needs for health and healing. It would be a scary world if man would have had no defense against disease and illness all these thousands of years. The ancients knew from the beginning the health secrets of the plant kingdom. Thanks to our loving Creator, eternal truth, such as is expressed in Ezekiel, is for our learning.

> And by the river on its bank, on one side
> and on the other, will grow all kinds of
> trees for food...their fruit will be for food
> and their leaves for healing.
>
> - Ezekiel 47:12 (NAS)

It is only a world ruled by money rather than by love that seeks to subvert this truth. Healing is a big part of what living is all about. How well we live our lives hinges on our acceptance or rejection of what God has revealed to us.

Over the centuries, the knowledge of essential oils was all but lost. When the library at Alexandria in ancient Egypt was burned and destroyed, hundreds of thousands of scrolls containing this knowledge were likely destroyed with it. It was not until the 20th century that the true healing power of essential oils became well known.

Today, we have stepped out of the dark ages in terms of re-discovering just how powerful and important essential oils really are to our health and well-being. But you are not likely to be treated with essential oils by a secular physician should you fall ill.

The pharmaceutical industry, which controls medicine in the U.S., cannot patent naturally occurring products. Without a patent, drug companies have no edge with which to compete. And so this marvelous, God-given gift is forsaken in modern medicine for the poisonous drugs we see today. However, the growing body of modern research that has developed regarding essential oil has not been lost.

Scientific research has demonstrated that essential oils are terminators of disease-causing micro-organisms. They are so deadly they can destroy them by proximity alone (This is due to the oil's volatility). Such notorious characters as staphylococcus, pneumococcus, meningococcus, hemolytic streptococcus, typhus bacillus, diphtheric bacillus, anthrax bacillus, Koch's bacillus, and many kinds of mold, have all been tested against and found subject to specific essential oils. The oil of oregano, for instance, is so powerful against microbes it can effectively sterilize raw sewage. Source: Jean Valnet, M.D., *The Practice of Aromatherapy*,

In 1985, Dr. Jean Claude Lapraz, M.D., one of the world's most respected and renown essential oil researchers, reported he could not find a single bacteria or virus that could live in the presence of the essential oils of cinnamon or oregano.

Perhaps most exciting, there is no known documented evidence of any pathogenic micro-organism (virus and bacterium) developing a resistance to essential oils! That is, **no micro-organism has been known to mutate to become immune to the oils**. This can mean only one thing: Essential oils are the perfect match to support and nourish our body's natural healing system. They are proving to be the missing link (God's provision) for which modern man has searched in order to bring about healing and vitality.

And finally, unlike pharmaceutical drugs, the American Association of Poison Control Centers reports zero deaths have occurred from using essential oils.

Chapter Six

How and Why Healing Oils Are Blessed by God For Healing The Sick

O nce you comprehend what follows will forever change your understanding of healing in the Body of Christ, His Church. There are two events recorded in Scripture, one in the OT, and one in the NT, that bind essential oils to the Church as God's blessing for us today.

In the Old Testament the Tabernacle served as a place of worship for the nation of Israel during their early history. God gave Moses very specific instructions on how the Tabernacle was to be built and used. In other words, It was to be a holy place. When it came time for the tabernacle to be open, God gave Moses the following instructions.

> Take the following fine spices – myrrh –
> cinnamon – cane – cassia - olive oil -
> Make these into a sacred anointing oil,
> a fragrant blend...Then use it to anoint
> The Tent of Meeting, the ark of the

> Testimony, the table and all its articles, the lamp stand and its accessories, the alter of incense, the alter of burnt offerings and its utensils, and the basin with its stand...**You shall consecrate them so they will be most holy**...
> Leviticus 30:22-29

Now come forward to the New Testament. In John 12 we read that Mary anointed the feet of Jesus (just prior to His persecution and death) with an expensive healing oil. She literally poured the oil on his feet and wiped His feet with her hair. When Judas Iscariot protested to her doing this Jesus said;

> "Leave her alone...**It was intended** that she should save this perfume for the day of my burial." - John 12:7.

Connecting These 2 Events:

As Christians, we know we are members of Christ's Body – Ephesians 5:30. In fact. a transliteration of that verse reads: "For we are members of his flesh and bones." Collectively our bodies comprise His Church, The Body of Christ- I Corinthians 3:16, 6:15.

Historically, the Tent of Meeting in the Old Testament served as an anti-type, a pattern or as a foreshadow of the New Testament Church (the Body of Christ) to come - Hebrews 10:1. So when God gave instructions to anoint the Tent of Meeting with essential oils, He was in effect giving instruction to anoint the Body of Christ.

When Mary anointed Jesus years later, she physically anointed the real thing (Jesus's physical body), what Old Testament priests could only symbolically anoint: The forerunner of the Body of Christ (His Church).

Under Old Testament law, no layperson could touch the oil used for anointing the Tent of Meeting, for it was sacred. Yet here is Mary, a layperson, anointing Jesus with a whole jar of precious oil and wiping His oil soaked feet with her hair. It was Mary's way of honoring or blessing Jesus for raising her dead brother (Lazarus) from the grave. However, in God's eye's, there is much more to Mary's act than what many Christians realize - John 12:7.

The Spiritual Connection:

What Mary did she did for herself, but God used the occasion to enjoin (bless) man's flesh with the flesh of His own Son: Something that had not happened previously. Mary's anointing of Jesus bonds all of humanity to the ultimate sacrifice Jesus Christ paid for our physical and spiritual healing - Isaiah 53:4-5.

God stipulated healing oils be used in the Tent of Meeting because they were ordained to be the natural counterpoint of Christ's divine healing ministry - Exodus 30:25, Acts 10:38.

Israel (Jacob) called essential oils some of the "best products of the land" - Genesis 43:11. And rightfully so. For they were valued for their natural healing qualities.

When Jesus, centuries later, received Mary's anointing of healing oil, He confirmed the sacred healing role essential oils hold for us today - John 12:7. Essential oils are the ordained physical counterpart of Christ's healing Body.

What is important here is to understand why essential oils were acknowledged in Holy Scripture, and set apart for use in the Disciples ministry of healing the sick - Mark 6:13; James 5:14.

God blessed essential oils and their use for healing, because these plant oils spiritually and physically bond mortal, corruptible human flesh to incorruptible, divine, eternal flesh in Jesus Christ. Essential oils serve as a reminder that it is God who is our Healer - Exodus 15:26.

Remember this truth and share it the next time you anoint a loved one with oil. People need to hear this story for edification, and to understand why it is anointing with essential oils are blessed by God for healing.

Healing In The School of Christ

When Jesus began His ministry, He proclaimed the Kingdom of God drawing near and healed the sick. Jesus never wavered in this teaching or practice.

Jesus saw Himself as being in conflict with evil, doing battle on a spiritual level made manifest in the physical world. He healed freely never asking what a person had done or how they had sinned. Only once did He warn someone not to sin again after He healed them -John 5:14. He recognized that evil (unclean spirits) can enter into our lives and body, given the best of intentions - Luke 11:24-26. He viewed the effects of unclean spirits (sin and sickness) in our lives as keeping us from reaching our full potential and calling.

This then sets the backdrop of what it was like to be a disciple in the School of Christ. The teaching and message is "God loves you." And what better way is there to demonstrate His love to you than for Him to heal you. This is the heart and soul of what the Incarnation of Christ is about - John 3:16-17, and what Jesus meant when He said the Kingdom of God is near you. It implies God breaking forth into the world and into the life of man to heal him from what evil has wrought.

Jesus Instructed the Twelve:

The chosen twelve disciples (Apostles) were with Jesus for most of three years. They were taught and prepared by Him to carry forth a message that would change the world – Mark 3:13-19. While we are not privy to every word Jesus spoke, through careful observation and deductive reasoning of God's Word, we learn essential healing oil played an active role in the disciples' healing ministry.

In Mark 6:7-13, we read Jesus sent the twelve out in 2 man teams on a kind of on-the-job training mission; for the ministry they would be doing after His departure. Before they went, He gave them very specific instructions. The results of their work is recorded in verse 13...

> "They drove out many demons and anointed
> many sick people with oil and healed them."

Before addressing the issue of the oil in the above passage, we need to first be clear about the healing performed. The Greek word used for "healed" in verse 13 is therapeuo, from which the English word "therapy" is derived. It literally means "to wait upon menially" (to serve), to "restore to health." So there be no question, therapeuo denotes the healing occurred over time. There is no indication the healings in verse 13 were in any way out of the ordinary or instantaneous. If the healings were instantaneous, the Koine Greek word, iaomai, as used in Luke 8:47, would have been used.

So we must (by using the rule of language) deduce the healings of Mark 6:13 occurred normally over a period of time. Were these healings divine? Yes! Were they miraculous? Yes, because all healing is divine by its nature and source.

What makes the healing reported in Mark 6:13 all the more curious is the healing modality employed by the twelve disciples. They anointed (applied with their hands) the sick with oil. The reason the oil is so interesting, so unexpected, is there is no previous passage that indicates the need or requirement to use oil in their ministry. The reader is suddenly left with their appearance. Consequently, without a previous text explaining the use of oil, the following questions are raised:

1. By whose authority were they using essential healing oils?
2. Where did the oil come from?
3. Why were the disciples using essential oil in their ministry?
4. What are it's implications for us today?

1. By Whose Authority Were They using Essential Oil?

As Mark 6:7-13 is read, it becomes apparent the twelve were under strict orders. Further, they were sent by twos. So, it is very unlikely all six pairs would "anoint sick people with oil" unless they had each received explicit instructions from Jesus, himself, to do so. To act without His word would have brought reprimand. We can deduce then, with assurance, that Jesus taught and authorized His disciples to anoint the sick with oil in their ministry, even though there is not a text saying He did so.

Further, they were "anointing" people. Anointing requires a learned procedure. This procedure, used by all six teams, would have required the same teacher in order for all twelve to be consistent in the manner they anointed. Jesus is the only teacher we know they had in common, so we can further deduce it was Jesus who taught them how to anoint.

2. Where Did the Oil Come From?

The ministry of Jesus demanded resources as any endeavor would today. It would need food, clothing, and shelter, obviously, but ministry supplies were also needed. How was the ministry supported to obtain those things it would need, like expensive healing oils?

Certainly, the support did not come by Jesus or His hand picked twelve. His disciples gave up all their worldly possessions in order to follow Him - Luke 5:11. How they were supported is found in Luke 8:1-3. A number of women of means (wealthy followers) supported the ministry. It was through their efforts that the ministry was furnished with supplies, including expensive healing oils.

3. Why Were the Disciples using Essential Oil in Their Ministry?

The answer to this question lies at the very core of Christ's teaching and mission. God's Scheme of Redemption is centered in the life, suffering, death, and resurrection of Jesus Christ, what the Apostles called the Gospel - I Corinthians 15:1-4).

The Gospel teaches us that all healing comes through our trust in Jesus, the first-born of the dead. In obeying the Gospel call, our old man of sin dies, and a new man, born of the Spirit of God, is given birth - John 3:5-7. In our spiritual rebirth our body no longer belongs to us; it belongs to Jesus Christ - I Corinthians 6:15. Our body spiritually becomes part of His body. This is what makes divine healing (both physically and emotionally) a reality.

In order for man's flesh to become one with God's flesh, God had to vanquish both sin and sickness from man's body and soul. To accomplish this feat Christ physically went to the grave bearing all of mankind's diseases, sicknesses, and infirmities, as well as sin - Isaiah 53:4-5. He literally became a sin offering - Isaiah 53:10. But even in death, Christ was busily at work. In death He carried all of mankind's grief's inflicted by Satan, and left them in the depths of hell. Christ then returned to the land of the living. Death could not hold Him because He, Himself, is without sin - Hebrews 4:15. In freeing Himself of our burdens in hell, Christ freed mankind from both his prison and prisoner forever - Luke 4:18.

When Satan deceived Adam and Eve in the Garden of Eden, he effectively had mankind pinned to the ground in sickness and death. No matter how hard man struggled to free himself spiritually from his evil conqueror, he was hopelessly lost. Unless

God could remove sin and sickness in man, God would lose his most beloved creation, His family of man. How God would free man from Satan was once a great mystery but now made known to all men - Romans 16:25-26, Eph. 3:6-9.

Sin and sickness no longer have dominion over man. Man is now victorious over Satan in Jesus Christ, our Lord and Savior. This was the primary teaching (the Gospel) the twelve Apostles shared with the known world during their entire ministry. <u>Repentance and healing were all part of the same message</u>. If you would like to do an interesting exercise, highlight the following verses in your Bible found in the Book of Acts of the Apostles. You will notice in each verse the same message is being shared— The Gospel!

Verses in the Book of Acts Common to The Gospel Message of The Apostles

2:23-28	4:10	10:39-40	17:18
2:31-32	4:12	11:14	17:31-32
3:15-16	5:29-30	13:36-37	24:15
4:2	8:35	14:7	26:22-23

The Greek word for salvation, soteria, pronounced "so-tay-ree'-ah," means rescue, or safety (physically or morally). The King James Bible uses salvation to mean deliver, health, salvation, save, saving. In other words, salvation is inclusive of physically healing our body, as well as our spirit and soul. This is the reason why crowds followed Jesus wherever He went. In Him is what every man alive wants—Healing!

Healing the sick was uppermost in the mind and ministry of Jesus. Divine healing provided a platform and great crowds for Him to speak about the Kingdom of God. The disciples witnessed Him in His work as a healer. They sat at His feet while He taught them about the Kingdom of God. He taught them how to pray and anoint using precious, healing oils. He authorized His disciples to drive out demons and sent them out among the people to experience their new found skills as healers. The necessary inference before us, then, is that it was Jesus who taught His disciples divine healing using essential healing oils.

If we can learn anything about Scripture, it is that nothing happens without a purpose. The precious healing oil we so casually read about in the Gospel of Mark is there for our learning.

In Scripture, God's perfect will is revealed in three ways: by command, by necessary inference, and by approved example. In the case of the disciples using essential oil in their ministry, we learn God's will through necessary inference and approved example.

Necessary inference carries more weight than approved example, but necessary inference is not the same as a command. In other words, there is no command from God telling us that we must use essential oils in healing the sick. James 5:14 is the closest statement we have to a command concerning the use of healing oil. But James 5:14 is not a command, it is an exhortation. The inference and example laid forth in Scripture, then, points us to a more excellent way. In following the example, we do not have to guess. We can read about essential healing oils in God's Word and know they are blessed by Him - Genesis 1:11-13 in healing the sick.

4. What Are The Implications For Us Today?

The implications of essential healing oils being used by the twelve Apostles as part and parcel of their ministry is enormous. First, it means that God, Himself, recognizes the excellence of essential healing oils and their superior healing qualities over man-made concoctions.

Secondly, the anointing of Jesus, Himself, with precious healing oil – Mark 14:3-9, denotes God's blessing for us to incorporate the use of healing oil in healing ministries - James

5:14. They confirm the healing union enjoyed between the Body of Jesus Christ and our body, spirit, and soul. This is why essential oils have God's blessing for the Church (the Body of Christ) to use in carrying forth its divine mission of divine healing.

Thirdly, where does all this leave us? Quite frankly, that is a question left to each of us to answer. For Christians who look to the Bible for a "Thus saith the Lord," they must examine preconceived doctrinal notions in light of this learned truth to see if these things are so. I hope they do. But as it stands now, most churches do not have a physical healing doctrine of which to speak. Many Church traditions speak of miracles (divine healing) in the past tense. They ignore God's love that wants to heal us here and now. God's no science approach to healing has simply been shelved and forgotten.

Chapter Seven

Living a Life of Health For God

The Role of Faith in Eating Healthy Food

As a believer in Jesus Christ, and student of God's Holy Word, you want to do all you can to live a life of holiness. That "all you can" part includes caring for your body, which belongs to God.

To be clear, you will not condemn yourself before God by eating at a fast food restaurant. That is not in the framework of discussion here at all. Rather, you want to do all you can to demonstrate your love to God by living a life of holiness.

When God issued His food law to Israel, He said the reason for observing these laws is to **consecrate ourselves to holiness** - Leviticus 11:44. Translated into modern English, that means eating healthy food should be a response to our faith. It arises naturally from our longing for obedience to God. It has nothing to do with the state of your soul...That is unless you knowingly violate your own conscience.

> I urge you, brothers, in view of God's mercy, to **offer you bodies as living**

sacrifices, holy and pleasing to God ---
This is your spiritual act of worship.
- Romans 12:1

We are told to offer our bodies as living sacrifices to God for good reason. Our bodies were purchased at great price by God - I Corinthians 6:20. As we grow in faith and knowledge of God, we begin to realize the importance of the kinds of food we eat. Is what we eat healthy or not? If not, why then do we continue to eat these harmful foods. These questions eventually come to all searching for a more excellent way. How we respond to those questions has to do with our growing in faith.

The Problem:

The Christian community, while strong on salvation, morality and Christian ethics, has had little to say about living a life of health for God (With emphasis placed on health for God rather than health for sake of health). Some churches offer various health-oriented classes, but again, the emphasis and motivation is often on health for one's own benefit, not necessarily for God. After doing several word searches on the Internet, I found few references on the subject.

While there are several reasons for this phenomenon, I strongly believe the primary reason lies with Church doctrines and the understanding of what is or isn't spiritual. The general concept of that understanding goes something like this: One looks to the Church for salvation, and to the world for health and healing. In other words, a large disconnect exists between how we think and treat our physical body as it relates to our Lord, Jesus Christ's body.

I believe some missing links in our walk with God include:

• Our lack of understanding of whom our body belongs to.

- How one's eating habit, diet and lifestyle is directly related to living a life of sacrifice.
- Our lack of awareness of the spiritual message our health (or lack of it) sends to those around us.
- Our lack of understanding that a large percentage of our health is directly related to the quality and quantity of food we eat.

Look around any Church and you will see Christians eat the same junk foods like most everyone else, drink the same soft drinks, get just as obese, come down with the same diseases and treated by doctors trained in the same medicine, take the same drugs and often die from complications following the same medications and treatment. This state of health in the Christian community speaks volumes about the Christian community at large.

That we as a community of believers overlook the importance of living for God in body is deeply disturbing. I am speaking about our eating and lifestyle habits, which are precursors to many diseases in our culture. If our body is a temple of God, then the quality and kinds of food we put into that temple should be very important to us – I Corinthians 6:19.

We should also be aware that God has given us all things that pertain to life and godliness - II Peter 1:3. But we seem not to be aware of "all" these things, and so we suffer.

Speaking spiritually, if we are willing to eat any and everything placed before us, and many do, I believe we are communicating the wrong message to the world. And as for those Christians who do eat healthy foods and exercise to stay fit for the sole purpose of increasing longevity, they too are missing the mark.

There is something more important than longevity: It is knowing God and doing His will. **We need to live for God, not for longevity.**

I believe God's perfect will is not that He heal the sick, but rather that we never get sick. I believe because our body is a temple of God, we should make every effort to remain healthy throughout our lives. In fact, our first priority as Christians should be to ourselves to live a life of health. This should be consciously and purposely pursued as a sacrifice and service to God. Only then can God be glorified in our body (Being a member of His fleshly Body).

Does this make sense to you? A healthy, physical Christian body glorifies God, but a diseased, or unhealthy body does not glorify God. Understand I am speaking of our physical body, not our faith.

God is glorified in healing, health, and life. Disease, sickness and death belong to Satan. This does not mean if your body is sick you cannot glorify God through other forms of service, it just means your body is under attack by what God calls unclean spirits.

However from the outside looking in, chronic sickness and disease in the Body of Christ makes His Church look no different from any other enterprise. People lost in sin who may know chronically ill Christians, often wrongly conclude their Church and faith is no different from any other enterprise: Like say the local gym.

Now there are lots of gyms and lots of churches. Think what it would mean if your church became known for all the healthy people that attend it. Think what it would mean if your local community connected your church to healing and good health. Do you think such awareness might draw more interest and increase attendance? Of course!

This is what makes Living a life of health for God all the more powerful. It's not just your voice and way of life, your physical well-being also bears witness to the life-saving power of the Gospel of Jesus Christ.

The purpose of this chapter is to help you grow spiritually in the Lord. The end result is intended not just to lead you to better

health, but to help you develop a closer relationship with God…
To know Him. I want you to understand how wonderfully you
were created and the love behind all that God provides for your
well-being.

Once this truth hits home and is weighed in our conscience,
there is only one thought that should occupy our minds about
our eating habits: How our diet affects giving glory to God.

Eating as An Act of Love.

Eating for many people is an egocentric act. That is, they eat
with only one thing in mind: To satisfy their hunger, a craving
unto themselves. It doesn't matter what it is they eat so long as
it tastes good. There is no sense of thanks giving or gratitude
expressed, only a gluttonous, solitary rush to fill up.

People who eat like this are reminiscent of pigs eating acorns
under a tree. Pigs never look up to acknowledge the tree that
provides the acorns. They only know there is food and lots of it.
This pig analogy is a reflection of the carnal world and how it
thinks and acts. Self-gratification rules the day.

Eating, of course, is a necessity and eating great tasting food
is a joy. There is no malcontent in either by itself. But carnal,
worldly-minded people go to the extreme and turn them both
into a lifestyle that is slowly killing them.

Why modern man suffers declining health:

The last 100 years of human development has brought many
changes, perhaps none more challenging than in the area of our
health. Of the many things that can impact human health, none
are greater than food and medicine. In this chapter we'll look in
more detail, and see how food has changed.

The majority of people today have no idea where their food
comes from. This is because the United States as a whole has
moved away from the traditional farming practices that our

ancestors thrived on, and turned to mega-farming factories instead.

One hundred and twenty years ago…

- Our great grandparents ate seasonal food, food grown locally.

- The average diet consisted of fresh and dried fruits, fresh and dried vegetables, wild grain and seeds, fish, raw unpasteurized dairy products, and meat from wild animals or locally grown livestock. The shelf life of most of these products was measured in days, weeks and months.

- The term "organic" was unknown, as all food was organic and people didn't think about it like we do today.

- Farmers grew diverse crops and replenished the soil with what came out of it.

- Farmers let land lie fallow so the land could rebuild itself with life-giving nutrients before replanting.

- Farmers saved seed from each crop for next year's planting.

- Animals were free range and fed on grass in pastures. Their waste helped those pastures grow and replenish nutrients.

- Ground beef consisted of meat from one cow.

- Meat and vegetables were preserved naturally.

Times have changed. Today…

- Produce and meat is shipped around the world. Food previously out of season can be bought in mega-grocery stores year-round.

- The average diet consists of highly refined, processed meats, fruits and vegetables, whose shelf life is measured in months and years.

- Dairy products are pasteurized and ultra pasteurized.

- The term "organic" refers to a specialty food.

- Single crop, large-scale farming operations that depend on chemical herbicides and pesticides, have replaced small, family owned farms.

- The land is fertilized with three inorganic chemicals, phosphorus, potassium, and nitrogen, forsaking all other vital soil elements.

- Land is not allowed to lie fallow.

- Farmers buy genetically modified seed resistant to Round-up pesticide. This means Round-up pesticide can be sprayed on crops to kill weeds without harming the crop...The same crop we eat.

- Animals are crammed together and fed in feedlots. They are given antibiotics and hormones to keep them from becoming sick and to make them grow as fast as possible.

- A pound of ground beef contains the meat from as many as 50 cattle.

- Fresh, canned and frozen food is radiated and preserved using chemicals.

The net result of these agricultural and food changes has brought on a whole host of new diseases not known 120 years ago. And every year new diseases are being diagnosed and named. The reason most of these diseases exist is due to our culture and diet. The very food we depend on to live has changed and is slowly killing us.

Unhealthy Food Additives:

Food producers have one thing in mind: To increase profits! One way they increase profits is by making food products taste good. By doing so they hope you will become a steady customer of their products. But if you buy food without reading the ingredient list, if you are not familiar with each ingredient, your long-term health is in jeopardy.

90% of all food found at your local grocer contains ingredients not fit for human consumption. These ingredients include mono-sodium glutamate (MSG), high fructose corn syrup, artificial sweeteners, trans fats, and nitrates to name just a few.

Commercially Processed Food is Not Food!

All commercially processed food contains "food products," food which is heavily processed. For the most part, food products are foods that are far removed from their natural state. To be accurate, the more a food is processed, the more it is NOT food. Your body was designed to eat natural, whole foods as they are found in nature, not artificial substances created in a lab. To compare the difference between natural, whole food and food products study the comparison below.

Natural whole food is:

- Grown
- Messy
- Variable quality
- Goes bad fast
- Requires preparation
- Vibrant colors, rich textures
- Naturally flavorful
- Strong connection to land and culture

While "Food products" are:

- Produced, manufactured
- Neat, convenient
- Always the same
- Keep forever
- Instant results
- Dull, bland
- Artificially flavored
- No connection to land or culture

Said another way:

- If it didn't exist until after 1903 (when the hydrogenation process was invented), it's probably not food.
- If it's wrapped in layers of plastic, cardboard and foil, it's probably not food.
- If it requires heavy advertising to sell, it's probably not food.

Avoid Commercially Processed Meat:

Hundreds of cancer researchers took part in a five-year project spanning more than 7,000 clinical studies designed to document the links between diet and cancer. Their conclusion, published in the World Cancer Research Fund's report, *Food, Nutrition, Physical Activity and the Prevention of Cancer: a Global Perspective. (2007)*, states that all people should immediately stop buying and eating processed meat products and that **all processed meat should be avoided for life!**

Processed meat has many ingredients and is usually packaged for long-term shelf life. These products almost always contain sodium nitrite, a cancer causing chemical additive used as a color fixer to turn meat products bright red. Here's a partial list of processed meat products that contain sodium nitrite:

- Bacon
- Sausage
- Pepperoni
- Beef Jerky
- All Deli meats
- Sandwich meat - including those served in restaurants.
- Meat gift products
- Meat in canned soups
- Lunch meat products
- Meat used in ravioli and spaghetti products

Two other unhealthy ingredients often found in processed meat includes monosodium glutamate (MSG) and processed salt.

If you want to avoid sodium nitrite in your meat diet, there are only two places in your grocer's store to find it:

1. In the fresh meat department where you find whole cuts of meat.
2. In the frozen food section where you can find nitrite free meat products. In all cases, read the food label when buying processed meat and look for sodium nitrite or sodium nitrate. If either of these ingredients is listed, DO

NOT BUY that product. Avoid these products for the health of your family.

Boycott these meats for life. This is not easy and requires understanding and a commitment from each family member. When you are at a pizza party, if there is meat on the pizza, do not eat it: Not because it is meat, but because the meat is most likely processed and contains sodium nitrite and MSG. Again, this is difficult, but necessary if you are committed to God and want to honor your body as a temple of the Lord. Anyone who knows about processed meat and continues to eat these products over the course of decades can expect to be eventually diagnosed with cancer.

Remember: Processed food of any kind is not really food at all.

The McDonald's French Fry Experiment:

Try this experiment at home. Buy an order of McDonald's French Fries. Next, peel and cut a potato into fries and fry them as you normally would. Third, place the McDonald's fries into a sealed glass container. Do the same with the homemade fries, dumping them into in a separate container. Mark the date on each container and set the containers on the counter out of the way. Keep the glass containers side by side exposed to daylight for 8 weeks, and watch the changes.

At the end of eight weeks, the McDonald fries will look the same as the day you put them into the container. The home-made fries will be blackened and covered with a fuzzy mold. Why is this?

While whole food in its natural state decomposes, processed food does not. So what does this experiment teach you? If the McDonald's fries do not decompose, of what good are they to eat? Your body CANNOT assimilate heavily processed foods - food that is not natural. This is why so many Americans are chronically ill.

"Every day, 7 percent of the U.S. population visits a McDonald's, and 20-25 percent eat fast food of some kind," says Steven Gortmaker, professor of society, human development, and health at the Harvard School of Public Health. As for children, 30 percent between the ages of 4 and 19 eat fast food on any given day.

But that's just the tip of the iceberg. About 90 percent of the money that Americans spend on food is processed foods. If you doubt that figure, the next time you are standing in the check out line at the grocery store, look at the grocery carts around you and notice all the cans, bags and boxes.

Think about it. If it comes in a box, can, or carton, it's processed. The fact that these foods are so readily available, and often of such poor quality; is why nearly two of every three Americans suffer from one or more chronic forms of illness.

The Food and Drug Administration (FDA) maintains a list of over 3,000 chemicals that are added to the processed food supply. These compounds do various things to food: add color, stabilize, texturize, preserve, sweeten, thicken, add flavor, soften, emulsify and more.

Some of these additives have never been tested for safety-- and require no government approval. Instead, they belong to the FDA's "Generally Recognized as Safe" (GRAS) list. An item is "safe," as defined by Congress, if there is "reasonable certainty that no harm will result from use of an additive." Are you willing to trust this nonsense with your life?

Healthy Food Alternatives:

Eat whole foods, foods that have not been processed, foods that are locally grown. Many locally grown vegetables, fruit and meat found at a farmer's markets are organic, even though the grower may not meet stringent organic standards to call their food organic. Never-the-less, most local growers rely on natural means to raise their crops. They rely on crop rotation, composting and other natural methods of farming. The beef, poultry and eggs they raise are grass fed and allowed to free range.

Best of all, you can talk to the grower and learn how they raised their food. You'll find this kind of shopping to be a wonderful experience.

Rediscover your kitchen and buy some food recipe books. Learn how to cook. I did. It really isn't hard and it is lots of fun.

Finally, avoid buying fast food. It may seem convenient, but convenience will not keep you healthy. But more than that...You harm your body each and every time you eat those french fries, burgers and fried chicken. They may smell delicious and look good, but they are not fit for consumption.

Church Fellowship Meals:

Chocolate cake and glazed doughnuts with coffee or pork BBQ and potato salad at your church's covered-dish supper may be comforting and scrumptious, but not generally considered healthy eating.

With fast food so easily available, rather than take time to prepare a dish with whole, fresh food, more and more of my brethren are buying and bringing fast food to Church potlucks.

These purchased dishes and drinks are laden with unhealthy food additives like MSG, trans fat, sodium nitrites, artificial sweeteners, and the like. It's not that our fellow sisters and brothers in the Lord don't care, they just don't know. And that presents a problem for those who do know.

Once you have determined to honor God in body through eating healthy food, what do you do in the food line at Church? The best choice may be to only eat what you prepared for the potluck. Potlucks can be tough.

This highlights the need and offers opportunity to discuss the role of faith in the foods we eat and why. But wait...Not so quick. While your neighbor seated next to you at the table is chowing down on a slice of Pizza Hut Pizza, he or she may not appreciate your words of wisdom. They are too absorbed in enjoying themselves and other discussions heard round the room.

A better way is to prepare and present your own choice of dishes on the food table. Home-made dishes stand out and are always a hit in today's fast food world, so why not start there to educate your Church family about eating as an act of faith. As people in the room begin to brag on your home-made dish, you will have their ear.

Here's a tip: You could make up a small placard with the recipe's name, and include a brief explanation of what makes your dish so healthy and place it next to your dish. People like that.

The point of this section is that many Church potlucks end up being a fast food nightmare. These events highlight a major problem and the need to warn and educate our brethren.

Epilogue

Nothing of God and faith you have read in this book makes earthly sense. That's because the intellect of this world pigeonholes the divine interaction of God in the affairs of man, so neither can it accept divine healing. Yet evidence of divine healing is all around us.

The problem for many believers in all of this is that the world still has its hold on them. Too many Church leaders today spend more time being doctrinally correct than they do being biblically correct. Divine healing is a problem for them, and many of us, because it operates outside of what the world is willing to believe. It is too risky. But until the Church moves beyond the world's intellect to the unseen world of God and Satan, until we come to know them both as the spiritual, dynamic entities that shape our lives, believers will continue to suffer with chronic illnesses and live unfulfilled lives.

We pay lip service to the unseen world of God yet force Him to operate by the world's standards. We want God, but we want Him in our pocket, limited and confined. Our faith is much easier this way. It is much easier to say God no longer heals than it is to have faith that He does. We are afraid God works and afraid He doesn't. It is as though we are beside ourselves, and so we continue to struggle in our faith.

> Where is the wise man? Where is the scholar Where is the philosopher of this age? Has not God made foolish the

wisdom of the world? For since in the wisdom of God the world through its wisdom did not know him, God was pleased through the foolishness of what was preached to save those who believe. Jews demand miraculous signs and Greeks look for wisdom, but we preach Christ crucified: A stumbling block to Jews and foolishness to gentiles, but to those whom God has called, both Jews and Greeks, Christ the power of God and the wisdom of God. For the foolishness of God is wiser than man's wisdom, and the weakness of God is stronger than man's strength.
- 1 Corinthians 1:20-25 (NIV)

It is the purpose of this book to strengthen your faith in the God of healing, to call the Body of Christ back to its mission of saving (healing) those in torment of Satan's devices. For this is the Body's divine calling. My hope is that you are edified in its reading.

The work of God has always been to restore that which Satan destroys. We are God's beloved children, made whole through the body and blood of Jesus Christ. We are empowered through Him and called to minister spiritual healing to the sick. Ours is not the luxury of whittling wood. We must meet the calling and do battle to be true to our Lord.

And now it is time to put this book to rest and give it over to Yahweh-Rapha. It belongs to Him now and to those who will have their hearts opened by its message. May the God of Healing, the God of Mercy, Love and Peace work in you always.

Amen!

Jim Lynn
Salem Mo
GodsHealingWord.org

Appendix A

Divine Healing Testimonials

Here are three very real life stories of healing that make no earthly sense. As you read them, notice how these people put their faith into action. The stories of these people reveal unquestioning faith, the kind of faith that Jesus said could move mountains - Mark 11:23. They tell more about God being in our lives than any book ever could. Their witness leaves the skeptic with no answers save one—Yahweh Rapha is the God who heals. Amen!

Prayer and Anointing With Oil Healed My Wife of Lung Cancer...Medically Documented.

My wife, Linda, was diagnosed with lung cancer in 1998. The x-ray showed a walnut size solid mass located in the upper lobe of the right lung, with tufts of finger-like growths extending all around the mass. The whole thing together looked to be the size of a man's fist. To eliminate the growth being a fungus, her surgeon ordered a blood test, which came back negative. He then said he was 90% certain the tumor was malignant.

Linda was immediately scheduled for lung surgery the following week. Her surgeon told us he would remove the upper half of her right lung and associated lymph glands. I remember as we drove home the day she was diagnosed that we were both in shock over this news. We were confident that the surgeon could do his job okay, but we had serious doubts about Linda possibly catching a staph infection while recovering in the Intensive Care Unit (ICU). Staph infections, which proves fatal in some cases, are common occurrences in ICU's. When we shared this concern with her surgeon, he told us the odds of Linda getting a staph infection in ICU were about 50/50. This was not acceptable to either of us. We also had doubts that surgery was the answer. After all, the cancer was a fleshly part of her body, not some foreign object lodged in her lungs.

Looking back, I can honestly say we were scared, not so much because of the cancer, but because we realized Linda was under spiritual attack. Praise God that we have spiritual weapons to fight back. Linda immediately gave her cancer over to Jesus Christ for healing.

We prayed fervently on the matter, and Linda did some needed spiritual house-cleaning. (She had held animosity toward her Mother). I then anointed her chest and upper back with a special blend of healing oils known for their support of the respiratory system. A friend of ours had previously told us about healing oils, and we had some on hand. I anointed Linda daily, using the oils, and prayed in the name of Jesus while anointing her.

A couple of days after learning of her cancer, Linda called the surgeon's office to decline the surgery. The surgeon's nurse did all she could to persuade her to re-consider, but Linda's faith remained strong. Two months to the day after the first x-ray was taken, Linda had another chest x-ray taken. Her surgeon had asked that she do this so he could "monitor the growth and progression of the tumor." But to the doctor's amazement, the tumor had shrunk in size. He was dumbfounded and said, while comparing the x-rays, "This doesn't happen without intervention."

Linda said back to him, "You're right, Doctor, it doesn't. We are praying, and my husband is anointing me with essential oils." Her surgeon simply smiled and said to "keep it up."

Back home we continued in prayer and anointing with oil. Two months later another x-ray revealed the tumor had shrunk even more—this time to the size of a pea. The entire floor of the clinic, housing several other doctor's offices and their staffs, by now had heard of the "miracle girl," as they called Linda. One nurse wept openly while hugging Linda. No one in this clinic had ever seen or heard of a lung tumor going into remission without medical intervention.

Today, March 22, 2000, a new x-ray showed no visible sign of the tumor. My wife's lungs are absolutely clear. Linda's surgeon, who never operated on her, told us this is the first time he had ever witnessed such a thing. I thought it odd he called it a thing and not a healing. He could not give any medical reason for what his eyes clearly told him had happened. He just kept looking at the collection of her x-rays and shaking his head as if in disbelief.

We give God praise, for we know it was He who intervened and healed her lungs. We also give credit to the healing oil. Not only did the oil have an apparent effect on Linda's tumor, it also allowed her to breathe much easier. Used together as a healing modality, we believe prayer, laying on of hands, and healing oils are without equal. We give God praise for His love and provision.

Linda's healing is medically recorded. Her medical records, including the xrays, are on file at Rockford Health Clinic in Rockford, Illinois. Her doctors are Dr. Rogers, Dr. Mellies, and Dr. William Sacksteder, her would-be surgeon, who I am certain must be sharing Linda's story with his fellows to this day. In praise of our Lord, forever!

Your brother in Jesus Christ,
Jim Lynn

A Dying Man Cries Out to God for Healing and Lives.

On June 12, 1994, at 7:00 EST, my lungs exploded, and blood gushed out of my mouth by the cupfuls. I thought I was drowning, and people who saw me thought I had been shot, as blood spewed out of my mouth. I could barely breathe.

Upon arrival at the hospital I was rushed into a special quarantined room, and a number of doctors and nurses began working on me. Everyone was afraid since they had no knowledge as to what was happening with me. On June 16, 1994, my doctor came to me and said that he did not believe that I would live another day since the bleeding in my lungs would not stop.

That night I decided to spend my last moments speaking to the Lord without the medical equipment that was attached to my body. I disconnected myself from the medical equipment and got down on my knees and began praying to the Lord.

I could not breathe once I got off of the machine and oxygen, but the Holy Spirit of Almighty God interceded on my behalf with words that I could not speak. Just before I was about to expire I cried out, "Lord, if I am to die, take me now, but if I am to live, then let me live."

This experience taught me how the Holy Spirit, who dwells in man can work for me through prayer. As I desperately tried to gasp for air the Lord immediately allowed me to breathe on my own.

That same night I made a covenant with Almighty God. I would spend the rest of my life spreading the Gospel of Jesus to all the world. The Lord has allowed me to keep that covenant by the creation and use of the first Internet Gateway to the world known as church-of-Christ.org and Internet Ministries.

The next morning my doctor and his team (five doctors) were amazed to see that I was still alive and now able to breathe on my own. After a battery of tests, my doctor concluded that I had a 90% chance of full recovery and that the bleeding had stopped, and not by his doing.

My doctor, being a Hindu, asked me for the name of my God. I responded by saying the Holy Scriptures identify Him by the name of Jehovah. My doctor then said, "Silbano, your God, Jehovah, is powerful, for it was He who healed you and not I."

The doctors kept me in the hospital for further observation, and after ten days they concluded that I had tuberculosis. This was incredible since I had not been coughing or even experiencing any type of illness. It felt as if the Devil had touched my lungs that June 12th evening. They kept me in the hospital for another month. From the beginning I believe that God healed me from that trauma. The State of Florida required me to take TB medication for about one year.

In late 1997 I moved to Dallas, Texas, and, by law, was required to report to the Health Department of the State of Texas. I became ill and thought I was going to die. My doctor, an elder of the church, sent me to the Health Department stating that I had TB. I had told this Christian doctor that God healed me of TB and that my problem had to be something else.

On the way to the Health Department I became dizzy and felt like fainting. Upon arrival, I was immediately taken in for x-rays. Later, in the head doctor's office, I was told that I have never had TB. I had a case of pneumonia in the lower left lobe of my lung, and my heart was weakened. This is what was causing the dizziness and fainting symptoms.

The doctor then had me admitted into Parkland Memorial Hospital where I spent three days recovering from pneumonia and heart condition. I was then given some heart medication and was told that I would have to take beta-blocker medication for the rest of my life.

I also prayed about this and asked the Lord to heal my heart, and he did. But just one week after taking the heart medication, I became ill with dizziness and returned to the hospital. There my doctor cut my heart medication in half. One month later the doctor said that he was taking me off of the heart medication since it was making me sick.

My doctor stated that he had never heard of anyone ever being released from taking this type of heart medication. To this day I have not had the flu, pneumonia, or any other type of illness, and my heart is working like that of a young athlete.

Post script:

The doctors found that my lungs were scarred and cratered from the trauma of bleeding internally on June 12, 1994. My doctors all stated that lung tissue will not regenerate itself and that I would have to live with scarred lung tissue for the rest of my life. This is what I was told on June 13, 1994, just one day after this traumatic episode.

In late 1997 the head doctor for the Department of Heath of the State of Texas in Dallas, Texas, showed me and a preacher friend my x-rays, and they were clean. According to the doctor, my lungs were in excellent condition, and there is no sign or evidence of ever having tuberculosis.

It is a great thing to know that God is alive and that He does answer our prayers. May the grace of God, the love of Jesus, and the peace of the Holy Spirit be with you and your family forever.

Your brother in Christ Jesus,
Silbano Garcia, II.
Evangelist
Church of Christ
Crystal City, TX

Bone Fracture Healing:

When our 33-year-old son was eight years old, he came into the house hopping on one foot and screaming in pain. I knew something was seriously wrong because this was a child who had a very high pain tolerance and seldom complained about anything ever hurting.

He plopped down in the chair next to "his books" and sobbed, "Mom, hand me my *Bible!* Nothing's wrong. Please don't call the Rescue Squad (911); just had me my *Bible*." He was sobbing hysterically but I couldn't get him to tell me what was wrong. Since it was obvious it related to his leg, I started to take off the cowboy boot on the leg he'd been favoring when he came in. He kept trying to prevent me from doing so! "Mom! Don't take off my boot! Nothing's wrong with my leg!!" When I got his boot half way off, I felt a shin bone sticking into my hand.

By this time, he was really protesting and getting wild so I yelled at him and said, "David! Stop that! Now you calm down right now!! You know that God isn't going to leave us just when we need Him the most!" Just as I said that, I felt the bone disappear and go back into place underneath my hand. He stopped crying and we looked at each other in amazement.

When I got his boot off, all that remained was a reddened area on his skin. I insisted that he stretch out in the lounge chair for a few minutes to calm down and to be sure he was okay, but in less than twenty minutes he was out playing again as though nothing had happened. After all these years, this still sends chills up my spine as I write about the events of that day!!

Suzanne S. Whitmire
Seneca, SC

Appendix B

The Big Stick Called Faith
By Jim Lynn

A Great Mystery:

I want to tell you about a great mystery that has perplexed Christians of our generation. This mystery has stirred doubt, fear and created unrest within the Church. What mystery am I speaking of? It is the mystery of the power of faith to heal the sick.

The mystery of the power of faith to heal the sick is not ours alone. For despite given the power and authority to drive out demons and heal the sick, the twelve disciples, themselves, struggled to administer that power and authority to the sick. In other words, the twelve handpicked men of Christ struggled with the issue of faith to heal the sick just as we do today!

Let's review some known facts:

We know Jesus sent His disciples out, two by two, to preach the kingdom of God and to heal the sick. But before doing so, He gave them each a huge stick to carry. That huge stick is God's authority and power - Matthew 10:1.

Armed with this big stick, the disciples were able to drive out demons and heal the sick of every known disease. Without the stick, these ordinary men were powerless.

But as we shall soon learn, just because these twelve were given God's power and authority to heal didn't mean they would always be successful. That's because Jesus required the twelve to possess one thing more, which only they themselves could supply.

What was that one thing you ask? **Faith!**

In spite of having God's power and authority to heal the sick, the disciples were powerless without their personal belief and faith that God would do as they asked of Him.

Mark 6:13 tells us when the disciples went out, they drove out many demons and healed the sick. Praise God! Imagine their joy and and the great enthusiasm which must have followed. They must have had many great stories to tell as a result. But wait:

On at least on one occasion, things didn't go so well. Not everyone was healed. The disciples had tried to drive a lunatic demon from a boy but were unsuccessful - Matthew 17:16.

When the boy's father related this information to Jesus, he replied, "O faithless and perverse generation...How long shall I put up with you?" - Matthew 17:17. Obviously, Jesus statement was not intended to be directed directly toward the disciples, although it most certainly included them.

When the disciples later came to Jesus in private to ask Him why they couldn't heal the boy, He answered them by saying, "because you have so little faith" - Matthew 17:19-20.

That's the mystery, the great mystery called faith, which the world fears yet today and has created division and strife within the Church.

Faith is the keystone that empowers God's authority and power to heal the sick. How much faith? Jesus said with just a little faith nothing will be impossible for you - Matthew 17:20-21.

Many years later, the Apostle James would admonish Church elders to pray over their sick in faith, and to anoint the sick with oil for healing - James 5:14-16. James had obviously learned the lesson of faith well from his own failure while in training with Jesus just years before. For he was with Jesus the day the father of the lunatic boy approached Jesus.

As previously stated: Faith in God's promise to heal is what separates men of faith in God, from carnal men who cower in fear or disbelief. This kind of faith is not intellectual or born of doctrine. It is a soul searching conviction (born of God's Word) which touches the very heart of God.

Church elders today, who dismiss James 5:14ff, of course do not practice James' admonition. To make themselves feel comfortable about their dismissal (and to be accepted by the world) they have Church doctrines which effectively puts God out of the healing business, and healing out of the Body of Christ (The Church).

The real question we should be asking ourselves is not whether God heals. The real question should be are we willing to believe and put our faith in God's promise to exercise His power and authority on our behalf?

That's a big question because faith to heal places God squarely into our midst, not far off in some unseen world. It puts Him right into our lives and world, much like our mother, father and children are part of our lives.

I have to tell you, many Christians are not comfortable with that thought. They fear God. They are more comfortable with a God that is somewhere over there, not here.

You see, faith for many Christians consists of believing in Jesus Christ as their Savior. That's good, but think about it. Faith to save one's soul is a far cry from faith that falls upon Jesus Christ for healing.

The former is benign and requires little beyond intellectual acceptance, kinda like acceptance that the earth spins one revolution every 24 hours on its axis. People accept the earth spins and go on with their lives. No biggy. We regulate our lives by this spinning, and that's about it.

Likewise, many people willingly conform their lives as Christians to live a moral existence with a hope for the resurrection. They count themselves faithful if they attend Church regularly, and do good works. That's the extent of faith for most Christians. Unless they are forced to renounce their faith or be killed, there is little to challenge their faith.

The latter, however, goes much farther. It actively calls upon God's power and authority with unwavering certainty to restore the human body to wholeness free of disease. That's not something the world (Satan) likes or accepts.

The implications of this kind of faith goes far beyond intellectual faith and being faithful to attend Church. This kind of faith stands squarely against the world and medical tests that says a person has cancer; and their doctor gives them two months to live. It defies Church doctrine which does not believe in divine healing. It falls with conviction and certainty upon an unseen all powerful God that He will fulfill His Word to us. That, friends, is the kind of faith Jesus had in mind when he lamented, "O faithless and perverse generation."

One of America's Presidents, Teddy Roosevelt, had a saying concerning America's role in the world. He said America should walk softly and carry a big stick. Of course, that big stick was America's military might.

As Christians, we are to walk softly and also carry a big stick, the big stick of faith that believes God's Word. That many Christians have entrusted the world to the care of their bodies at the expense of forsaking God's power and authority to heal speaks volumes about the size of the stick they carry.

Appendix C

Ask Your Doctor to Wash Their Hands
By Jim Lynn

One hundred and seventy years ago (1850's), one of every eight mothers admitted to the University of Vienna for delivery of babies were leaving in caskets. Dr. Ignaz Semmelweis, head of the maternity ward, wanted to know why.

Dr. Semmelweis noticed the women were dying from the same disease that physicians and medical students had been studying in the morgue in-between giving pelvic exams. He also noted the women who received pelvic exams were more likely to fall ill than those who did not.

Semmelweis then concluded, years before the establishment of germ theory of disease, that the doctors and medical students were inadvertently killing mothers of new born by transmitting some invisible agent of the disease during prenatal exams. After the corpse of a woman was removed to the morgue, the agents that killed her were passed back to the maternity ward on the hands of medical personnel and then passed from patient to patient.

To break this cycle, Semmelweis introduced the practice of hand-washing with a chlorine disinfectant. This treatment was followed by an application of oil to the hands to serve as a barrier to any organisms remaining on the hands.

Within months, Semmelweis's simple solution cut the mortality rate in the maternity ward from 1 in 8 to 1 in 30. (*Plague Time, Paul Ewald, Anchor Books, 2002*)

Today, germ theory of disease is well-known by every first year medical student, and it is taught in every U.S. medical university. But what good has it done?

In 1991 a study of a nursery ward for newborns in Chicago showed that nurses followed appropriate hand-washing guidelines about half the time; doctors followed the same guidelines at about one fourth of the time. (*Plague Time, Paul Ewald, Anchor Books, 2002*)

Now This:

A recent investigation conducted by the Chicago Tribune found that more than 100,000 deaths in the year 2000 were linked to infections that patients received in our nation's hospitals. (*Dirty Hospitals: Are Hospitals Spreading Germs to Patients?, Chicago Tribune, July 24, 2002*)

Do physicians and hospitals really care?

The Tribune report found that nearly three-quarters of the deadly infections, or about 75,000, were preventable because they were caused by unsanitary facilities, germ-infected instruments, unwashed hands, or other lapses. Why?

Only 50 percent of medical personnel make time to wash their hands.

Many hospitals do not clean rooms between patient admissions. Common sense dictates that germs from the last patient will still be evident in the room unless it is properly disinfected. Contamination occurs from clothing, blankets, bed rails, walls, electronic thermometers, sinks, showers, tubes which are inserted into the body, gloves worn by health care workers, and improper ventilation systems.

Doctors and nurses wear their scrubs to work, then walk right into the operating room. Nothing like saving time to be able to see more patients.

Some doctors do not wash their hands before surgery because they are wearing gloves, forgetting that they are using their dirty hands to put on those gloves. Moving from patient to patient, they do not bother to wash their hands, and only put on gloves for surgery because hospital protocol dictates that they do.

Deaths linked to hospital infections represent the fourth-leading cause of mortality among Americans, behind heart disease, cancer, and strokes. These infections kill more people each year than car accidents, fires and drowning combined.

It could be argued that medical personnel simply place more reliance on antibiotics than they do on hygiene, but that is simply not true. They know what works and why? To side-step one of the most basic, elementary hygiene protocols is crass and a flagrant disregard for patient health. The reason hospitals and physicians do not make time to sanitize rooms, equipment, hands, etc. boils down to money. "Patient care" has become lip service, not a mandate.

Patients have a right to demand that hospital staff workers and their physicians wash their hands before touching them or anything in their hospital room.

During clinic visits, note whether your doctor washes his/her hands before examination. There are sinks and anti-bacterial soaps in every exam room. If your doctor simply puts on latex gloves, ask that they first wash their hands.

Doctors, clinic and hospital staff members all know the importance of good hygiene in controlling infections. They know they are suppose to wash their hands before they touch you, but most do not. Your health is more important than their time. And as they are working for you, you have a right to demand that they wash their hands.

How far have we come in medical care? Well, you be the judge. Many will say we have come far. But what if those who died from pathogens passed on to them by their physician could speak? How would they answer?

Appendix D

If I Were Satan
By Jim Lynn

If you were Satan, what are the two institutions you could attack that would destroy more lives than wars and natural disasters combined? Here's what I would do:

Phase One: Medicine

If I were Satan, I would **capture the medical industry** and make it mine. For what other of man's institutions could potentially inflict more harm? I would **infiltrate medical colleges** and teach students to treat disease symptoms, rather then teach them how to heal the sick.

I would **teach medical students that chronic disease is the result of natural manifestation**, and disclaim any correlation between disease and one's spiritual state of being.

I would **create chemical drugs with lethal side effects**, and tell medical students they must use only my drugs to treat their patients disease symptoms. I would **tell students that natural substances can be harmful** to the body and should not be used or trusted for treatment of the sick.

I would find greedy men who could care less about the well-being of people, and **set up a drug enterprise designed to keep sick people sick**. I would advertise my drugs on TV so people will ask their doctors to prescribe them.

I would take natural body conditions like, acid reflux, hormonal imbalance, sinus infections, high blood pressure, digestive disorders, osteoporosis, diabetes and **make them a disease**. That way, I could find more uses for my drugs.

I would be clever when using medical terms, so **people will begin to believe their body cannot be trusted**. I would use terms like, heart attack, spastic colon, and kidney failure.

Next I would **mislead patients into believing they have a disease** discovered through diagnosis; when in truth all they received is a specific diagnosis with a name. This will make it sound like the doctor has found a disease, and people can be "diagnosed" just in time to take a new drug of mine for the rest of their life.

Next I would **use man's government to protect my medical interests and drug industry**. I would set up a Food and Drug Administration, and use it to deny citizens any form of real healing. I would use this FDA to my advantage by making it unlawful for anyone to make health claims without scientific proof. Of course, I would also control the researchers, and medical doctors who publish results of research, so results are kept in my favor.

I would **refuse my agents to investigate any claims** that suggest a correlation between vaccines and disease and death rates.

Phase Two: Church

If I were Satan, I would **fill pulpits in churches with pastors who teach that God no longer heals the sick** like people read about in the Bible. I would have these pastors teach that healing must be instantaneous to be called a miracle.

If I were Satan, I would **convince God's people sickness and disease is the result of natural manifestation, not spiritual manifestation**.

I would **change the original meaning of the words "heal," and "save"** recorded in the Bible, so their true meaning and application is not understood.

If I were Satan **I would have church Pastors and teachers ignore the Old Testament**. In this way Christians will not know who God as: Their Healer, their Provider, Their Shepherd, their Redeemer, their righteousness, their Peace, their Lord of Lords, the Lord who makes man holy.

I would **put fear of persecution and public ridicule** in the hearts of church leaders were they to teach that God actively intervenes in this physical world.

In this way I can **deny God's glory of healing** by those who bear the mark of His Spirit and wear the name of His Son.

The End Result:

Over time, there will be very little knowledgeable and effective spiritual resistance to my sin induced sicknesses and disease. People will come to put more faith in medical knowledge than in the God of knowledge.

In this way, I can kill many millions of people because most people are raised up to respect the word and advise of medical doctors and preachers.

If I were Satan and wanted to destroy as many lives as I could, this is what I would do and how I would do it.

> For our struggle is not against flesh and blood, but against the rulers against the authorities, against the powers of this dark world and against the spiritual forces of evil in the heavenly realms. Therefore put on the full armor of God, so that when the day of evil comes, you may be able to stand your ground, and after you have done everything, to stand. - Ephesians 6:12-13

Put God back into healing and healing back into the Church (the Body of Christ).

Visit **GodsHealingWord.org**

Appendix E

Questions and Answers

Some years ago I was invited to answer questions concerning God's Healing Word ministry with a Christian online social media group. Doing so helped many readers to better understand God's Word. It also helped me to better explain this very important subject in our lives. What follows are just a few examples of comments and questions of over 60 submitted and my reply. I offer them here to help readers understand the confusion we (myself included) often have with our conception (belief) of biblical truth.

Tina comments:

- If I stopped taking my medicine I would be quite
- ill within two days, hospitalized within a week,
- dead in a year. They say the Serevent I take
- has killed people, but it works great for me.
- I also take an inhaled steroid every day.

She also asks:

1. Why are babies born sick when they have no sins?
2. Why are we not healed of all sickness when we are baptized?

My reply:

My Sister,

My heart goes out to you. I could not answer your questions, without first addressing your physical need. Know this, Tina.

Taking drugs like Serevent and steroids every day is not normal. You were not born to depend on drugs to breathe.

My remarks here will be brief. You will need more knowledge and spiritual help to break the dependency you now have on these drugs.

A condition described as cell wall rigidity prevents the process of osmosis necessary for normal cell function. With asthma there is stiffening of the cell walls of the alveoli. This causes carbon dioxide to become trapped and excludes oxygen. So you have breathing problems, and find yourself gasping for air.

Drugs like Serevent relax the cell walls so that the carbon dioxide can be released, and oxygen starts to be absorbed.

Conventional medical wisdom has been that cell wall rigidity is caused by exposure to allergens, dust, dander, etc. However, John Hopkins University research has proven that nothing we breathe can cause an asthma attack.

Christians versed in spiritual healing know that asthma is a fear-anxiety manifestation caused by spiritual forces, not physical. In this case it is the spirit of fear that is is able to control our physiology through the hypothalamus gland.

Spiritual healing ministries are trained to root out these unclean spirits behind physical suffering. We know for instance, that in many cases, not all, the fear of abandonment and resulting insecurities are key issues behind asthma.

A well trained spiritual healing team, through loving consulting, can expose such fears, perhaps laid deep within our subconscious, and administer healing.

The problem with medically prescribed drugs is that while they may relieve symptoms, they do not and cannot heal the person of whatever medical condition they may suffer from. And this is where secular medicine is today: It treats and manages, it does not heal.

I have much more to say about living (relying on) drugs and secular medicine in my book, *The Miracle of Healing in Your Church Today*. Now to your two questions:

1. Why are babies born sick when they have no sins?

Think back to Genesis when sin entered the world. Sin changed the world God created. Sin is why babies are born sick, not that they themselves sinned. We live in a world permeated with sin, it reaches into every aspect of nature, including the DNA of human, animals and plants. (Compare Genesis 3:17ff with Romans 8:19-21) Sin is behind every suffering you can think of.

2. Why are we not healed of all sickness when we are baptized?

Salvation through baptism is a legal act – Acts 2:38-39. Sanctification (righteousness) is a life long process which happens after baptism. This accounts for why we read such verses as Romans 7:14-25, I John 1:5-10.

Said another way, though spiritually reborn, we are still the same person emotionally, with our habits and feelings unchanged. Unclean spirits can live in our hearts right along with the Spirit of God. One or the other will prevail. It is us who decides which spirit prevails.

I hope this helps. God truly has the answers to our health issues. See Proverbs 4:20-22.

Jim Lynn

Rudy writes:

- What Paul writes in Ephesians 6 is, again, not
- what you claim. Is there a spiritual battle going on?
- You bet! But this battle is not fought out in our
- physical bodies! This battle is fought over our
- SPIRITUAL well being, our souls!

My reply:

I want to thank you, Rudy, for supplying statements like the one above. It illustrates the need to better understand why <u>man would not be man without his body, spirit, and soul joined together as one</u>; and how the Gospel event works to both save and heal (body, spirit and soul).

This will be short.

We are in agreement that this spiritual battle is for our soul. But have you considered how it is to Satan's benefit to sicken God's people?

Lastly, considering your statement above, would you please explain to me your understanding of:

1: Why God created man with a physical body.
2: Why Jesus Christ lives in the flesh as a man.
2: Why God calls himself Yahweh-Rapha.
3: Isaiah 53:4-5
4: Psalm 103:2-4
5: James 5:13-16
6: I Peter 2:24

Jim Lynn
GodsHealingWord.org

David writes:

- Brother Lynn, would chronic depression be
- caused by unclean spirits?

My reply:

Hi David,

Thank you for the question.

Professional medics tell us that depression is the result of a chemical imbalance in the body. It can be caused by either drugs, or by the over or under production of normal neuro-transmitters that are manufactured by the body.

A lack of self-esteem is the root cause of depression. Lack of self-esteem, self-rejection, self hatred, and guilt are all very damaging to the human spirit.

The limbic system is the connection between thought and the body. It connects to the hypothalamus gland, which is the responder to thought. Between the limbic system and the hypothalamus gland, they control the functions of the body.

In the case of low self-esteem, the body responds with a drop in serotonin in the brain. This is where the chemical imbalance comes into play with chronic low self-esteem.

Secularists will say the lack of self-esteem stems from mental belief, and that is true clinically. But as everyone knows, belief such as in self-esteem is made by us in the heart (reference Proverbs 4:23).

What many Christians seemingly are not aware of is that it is the heart where God and Satan do battle for our souls. In other words it is the heart that is the body's door to the spiritual world – Proverbs 4:23.

Christians know Satan is the father of lies. Satan does his bidding of lies in the heart. The choices we make from the heart are based on what we are willing to believe or reject.

Another spiritual factor about self-esteem is how we were nurtured by our parents and treated by relatives and acquaintances as adolescents. Nurturing is an external factor, which Satan also uses to his advantage.

Sometimes lack of self-esteem can be inherited because it has been there from generation to generation.

The bottom line is that whether attacked externally through lack of nurturing or internally through a spirit of Satan, it is the heart where judgment and belief is held.

So to answer your question: Yes, depression can be the result of unclean spirits.

Jim Lynn

Kim writes:

- You said also that all healing is spiritual in nature
- and that without the suffering death, burial
- and resurrection of Jesus Christ from grave,
- there could be no healing. I do not understand
- that comment at all. I hope my questions do
- not anger you.

My reply:

Kim,

No, your questions do not anger me. Why should they? I welcome them.

Let me explain why and how the Gospel of Jesus Christ is the key to all healing, both physical and spiritual, from creation to today.

It's perfectly natural for humans to think in terms of time. But time exists only within the created, material universe. There is no such thing as elapse of time, a beginning of time or end of time in the spiritual realm of heaven.

God sees events in time (our world) as happening all at one time. As many times as I have stated that truth, I still find it hard, myself, to wrap my mind around the concept of a timeless eternity.

God has no beginning or end. He just is. I think that's one reason He refers to himself as "I am that I am."

Now notice how God describes Jesus in Colossians 1:15-17 in both the past and present tense.

"He is the image of the invisible God, the firstborn over all creation. For by him all things were created: Things in heaven and on earth, visible and invisible....All things were created by him and for him. He is before all things, and in him all things hold together."

Every time I read those verses and contemplate their meaning, I am in awe. Do we really grab the full meaning of those verses? I think many do not. The meaning of those words is so grand, so spectacular, so out of this world, our fallible, corruptible brains simply want to skip over their meaning.

What I understand Colossians 1:15-17 to say is this:

Jesus Christ is fully human and God at the same time.

From the foundation of the world, God saw Jesus on the cross and His resurrection (The Gospel event). It was a done deal to Him, even though that event happened in time thousands of years (in time) after creation.

Without the Gospel event, life would cease to exist. Even the grass we walk on would die. Why? "...in him (Jesus) all things hold together."

Without the Gospel event, healing of any kind would not exist. The simplest cut on your finger would never heal. Why? "...in him (Jesus) all things hold together."

All of life, including healing, must (by definition) be actively divine and spiritual in nature. To think otherwise is to believe a lie of Satan.

That a cut seemingly heals by itself is <u>an act of active divine healing</u>. That nature recovers from its own disasters is an act of active divine healing.

Every breath of air we inhale and every blink of the eye are acts of divine love sustained in the person of Jesus Christ. Praise God! That we should believe otherwise shows what great influence Satan has in the hearts of mankind.

Before the Gospel event occurred, all of nature and mankind were sustained by the promise of God for a deliverer (Genesis 3:15). After the Gospel event occurred, all of nature and mankind are sustained by the promise fulfilled.

Now many would call natural healing an act of providence. Maybe so, but to me using the term providence falls short of understanding the whole story. This is why I use the term "an act of active divine healing."

This is how the healing process can exist in nature both physically and spiritually. For everything hangs on Jesus Christ and Him crucified for our sins and infirmities (Isaiah 53:4-5).

Jim Lynn
GodsHealingWord.org

Printed in the United States
by Baker & Taylor Publisher Services